To Rosemary

best wi

Memoirs of a Bow Belle

Memoirs of a Bow Belle

Billie Holmes

The Pentland Press Limited
Edinburgh • Cambridge • Durham

First published in 1995 by
The Pentland Press Ltd.
1 Hutton Close
South Church
Bishop Auckland
Durham

ISBN 1 85821 247 2

Typeset by CBS, Felixstowe, Suffolk
Printed and bound by Antony Rowe Ltd., Chippenham

Dedicated to my friend,
Lisa Cox

Preface

I would like to thank my grandson Richard Easter, script writer for the BBC, for giving me the idea and encouragement to write this book. Also, my son-in-law Allan for typing out the manuscript.

Chapter 1

On 7 April 1914 a scrap of humanity was born in a two-up two-down terraced house in Bow in the East End of London. That scrap was me, christened Agnes after my mother.

My father was an electrician working for the Poplar Borough Council. In August, war was declared against Germany. Early in the new year my father enlisted in the Royal Engineers.

I obviously don't remember an awful lot about the war. I do remember, though, the Boy Scouts coming round on their bikes yelling 'Take cover!' When all was clear they came round ringing bells.

I also remember one night when my mother's father was visiting us, he was holding me in his arms at the front door showing me the stars. To our amazement we saw this great Zeppelin balloon in the sky. The next second it exploded into flames. The impact threw Granddad several yards into the house, throwing me to the ground. Luckily we were not injured, only badly bruised, but I was very frightened indeed. I think my fear of the dark in later life sprang from this shock.

After this, whenever there was a raid, we would go down in the cellars of St Andrew's Hospital which was about five minutes away. I can still recall how frightening it was; hundreds of people outside the big iron gates to the entrance of the hospital, pushing and screaming. When the gates were opened all those in front fell inwards, it was horrible. At last we would all get in and settle in the cellars, wondering what we would find when we went up again.

Time went on, and like everyone else my mother was having trouble making ends meet, so she went back to work. Before her marriage she was a french polisher for Mason Pearson who made beautiful hair brushes.

This time, however, she worked for the undertaker polishing coffins. I'm horrified now but it didn't mean a thing to me then.

Some time later my grandfather died. Funerals in those days were dignified affairs. Beautiful glass hearse on an elegant carriage pulled by sleek black horses, carrying purple plumes on their heads. Such calm, such dignity. All the houses in the street would have their curtains drawn. Neighbours collected for a wreath. As the cortège went slowly by every man raised his hat.

My grandmother was now alone so Mother and I moved in with her at No. 17 Powis Road, Bow, E3. They were cottage-type houses with the front door opening on the street.

My mother, like all the other women, whitened her front steps; they were kept immaculate. No back gardens, just a 'yard' with an outdoor toilet. My mother, who loved growing things, had pots hanging on every bit of wall she could find. It used to look very nice actually. Having no gardens, the children had to play in the street. There was hardly any traffic, only men with wheelbarrows or a horse and cart selling things.

We also had a 'Bobby' policeman patrolling the street and everybody loved him. Cricket and football were played in the road. Marbles and hopscotch, 'Jacks' as well. Mostly girls did skipping, ring of roses, top spinning and bowling hoops. 'He' was my favourite game.

I liked living in Powis Road but suffered agony every night when I wanted to 'spend a penny'. I used to sit and pray that some one else also wanted to go, so that I could go out with them. After a while my dear mother realized I was afraid of the dark and would come out with me, and stand sometimes in the pouring rain waiting to take me back to the house.

I had started going to school now at 'High Street School for Girls' where I made some friends. Rene Cole, a ginger-haired girl, Sissie and Edie Sampson, two sisters, and a boy named Jimmy Bettis who lived three houses away from me.

My mother took me to school the first two mornings, then Jimmy's mother suggested, as he was two years older, he could take me and bring me home. Jimmy was taking me everywhere with him. All his exploits with the other boys had me tagging along.

One afternoon I could not be found, but was eventually caught trying to climb a tree with two young boys pushing me up by my bottom! The friend of my mother's who found me brought me back home, remarking to my mother that I was a regular 'William' [the naughty boy in the *Just William* books]. I was called William for some time but it was shortened to Billie quite soon. The nickname has been mine ever since.

The boys' school was at the back of the girls'. Rene, Sissie and Edie were all in the same class with me. We were very nervous, very conscious of our clean 'pinnies' and shiny black boots. I loved school but hated wearing the lace-up boots all children wore in the Twenties. Thank goodness for Sundays; I had boots with buttons up the side!

My father did all our boot repairs. He had an iron last and would buy a piece of leather from Petticoat Lane Market. I used to love watching him cut a shape out. For school we had metal tips on the toes of the boots, otherwise we wore them out in no time at all.

We had not been at school long before the Armistice was signed and our dads came home. I remember all the parties and celebrations, but felt very sad, for we knew lots of families who had lost someone, or some that had returned badly wounded or shell-shocked.

After my father's return from the war, he was awarded the Military Medal for Conspicuous Bravery in the Field. A piece was written in the newspaper about his exploits. I still have the Military Medal and am still very proud of him. Apparently he took a party of men into 'no-man's-land' to lay telephone wires. They were shelled and gunned down. My father dragged his companion, who was wounded, to safety, then went back for the others, hence the medal!

He returned to his job as an electrician and life went on again. Soon after this there was an epidemic of scarlet fever. Children under-nourished by war were catching everything. Two little girls I knew died. Another little friend was paralysed and was being pushed around on an iron stretcher. Many children had rickets, it was pitiful.

So many men were unemployed; these very men who had fought for their country, giving life and limb, feeling lost and unwanted. Even as a little girl I felt so angry that no one seemed to care about them!

I had gone to bed one night to be awakened by noise and unusual goings on. I got out of bed to investigate and was told I now had a little sister. I promptly said, 'Send her away, I don't want her!' But of course when I saw her, I loved her. She was named Veronica, which was soon shortened to Vera. Life continued very happily, me loving the baby more each day, until I awoke feeling ill one morning and it was found that I had scarlet fever. I was taken away to the Fever Hospital at a place called Homerton. I remember the ambulance went through the Blackwall Tunnel.

To my mother's horror they took baby Vera too as I had been in close contact with her. Fortunately after a week they sent Vera home, but I was to remain away for two months, as the fever had affected a valve in my heart. I quite enjoyed my stay at hospital after the first couple of weeks. The nurses made a fuss of me. One I liked in particular as she always found me some pretty ribbons to tie back my dark, curly hair.

At last I returned home, but mother was advised to take me to the London Hospital in Whitechapel Road. A surprise awaited me the first night home. Up in my tiny bedroom which had been, in my fantasies, palace, castle, stage etc., a big change had been made. My sister's cot had been placed where my bed had been. My bed now was a mattress placed on the floor in the nook for me to sleep on. Now the 'nook', so called, was like a very deep cupboard in the wall, about five feet long and four feet deep, but the bottom half was filled in up to three feet, which meant you had to stand on a box or a chair to get in.

Some exciting games had been played in here by me and some of my friends, but to sleep there was a very different thing. However, after a couple of nights I had thought of ways to improve matters. I asked Mother if I could have a curtain put up cutting me off from the rest of the room. I found a little low stool to put beside the mattress as a table, with a candlestick and a flower stuck in an egg cup. I was really getting excited with my half room. Draw the curtains and I had a secret place! Dad made a three-step stool for me to step up and down. I really began to love it.

I was seven years old now and had been going to Sunday school since I was five, so now Mother thought I could go to Bible Class. We were a

Methodist family and our chapel was a place called 'Central Hall', the Reverend Harry Williams our Minister. He had served as a Padre in the war so we all called him 'Padre'. He was a darling, about six feet two inches, a big frame, and a jolly laughing face, so very kind. After evening chapel down in the basement, which was very large, he held a social hour. Cups of tea were given and the men were given tobacco for their pipes. Sometimes the Padre would recite poems, and at others his niece Miss Sally, who was a school teacher, would sing; she had a beautiful voice. The church choir would often sing too. I used to come to these meetings and Sunday to me was the best day of the week.

At Sunday school in the afternoon, we heard wonderful stories from the Bible and were given pretty coloured texts. I also enjoyed the hymn-singing. Miss Sally was my Sunday-school teacher, and she listened to my singing and asked my father if he would object to her giving me singing lessons.

All this while our house was lit by gas. We had brackets projecting from the walls with a gas mantle to light for a flame. We had pretty glass shades; usually there were one each side of the mantle piece.

In our scullery we had a stone copper with a fire underneath. When this was lit we boiled the washing in the copper! Mother used a 'dolly' to push the washing around. After that the clothes were put through a mangle turned by hand, with a pail to catch the water.

At Christmas time we had a chicken for dinner. Such a luxury. We never aspired to a turkey. We only saw those hanging in the butcher's or in pictures! Mum usually managed a piece of beef from her brother's for Boxing Day. She started her Christmas pudding in October and would make about four of them. They would be steamed for hours and hours.

All our Christmas chain decorations were made at home; strips of coloured paper stuck into rolls and looped into one another. These were looped over pictures and across ceilings. We always had a tree. The ornaments came out every year more tattered each time but were usually cheered up by new tinsel.

Christmas night all the family of aunts and uncles came, and we had a super party. For entertainment there was me at the piano, Dad on a trumpet of sorts, Mother with a comb and tissue paper, kids banging on a tin box with a wooden spoon or two tin lids bashed together. If you were lucky you got a turn on Mother's precious tambourine! Such a din! We all loved it. This indeed was Christmas!

A couple of years went by with me doing most of the things that children do. I loved school; history, English and art being my favourite lessons. The main dislike was not being able to do 'Drill', which I would have liked to have done. Also no running or jumping. I had to attend once a fortnight at the London Hospital and had to take horrible medicine.

When my father returned from the war he received a gratuity. Not a large sum, but to us it was like riches. He had always wanted to own a plot of land, his 'little bit of England'. Somewhere he had heard of a place called Canvey Island in the Thames Estuary. So one Saturday we all set off to Southend hoping to get a boat to take us across to the Island and we found a boatman doing trips.

Off we set, but I think the boatman was making his first trip also. He didn't seem to know where to land, but took us as near as he could to the seawall. He put a plank across and said 'It's the best I can do.' For a moment everyone sat still, then with a lot of grumbling, we all began to move. Besides our little family, there were four other people on board. My father got off first, then helped my mother who was carrying my little sister. I brought up the rear. I think I was the only one enjoying it!

We found we were at the foot of a seawall, so after making sure the boat would be there to take us back we set off. Going we knew not where! A few minutes after starting to walk, down came the rain! Slipping and sliding on the muddy seawall. The women grumbling, my mother in particular saying, 'I never wanted to come here in the first place.'

We all trudged along wet and miserable in single file, a bedraggled lot. It's very funny now, but was not so funny then. Eventually Dad found a path leading down from the wall to an unmade track; one couldn't call it a road. After quite a trek we found a little shop. Hoorah, civilization! Dad went in and inquired where the High Street was and was told – this is it!

A little further on we found another hut which was an estate agent's office. Dad inquired about the plots of land he had seen advertised. After some discussion he found he had enough money to buy four plots, large enough for a bungalow and decent garden. Mr Price Powell the estate agent gave us the name of a builder's merchants on the Island who would fence the plots off for us. The name was 'Holmes Bros'. Little did I know how involved I would become.

Having arranged all the business, we set off to find the boat. I shall never forget that day's outing. Mother swore she would never set foot on that dreadful place again. My poor darling dad. I was thrilled for him. He stuck to his guns. Every so often while he was saving up to buy materials for the building, he would go to the Island to check no one had stolen his precious plots.

In those days there were only about three farms and a dozen or so houses, including the 'Dutch Cottage', there. Dad had found a new way of getting there. He took a train from Barking to Benfleet and either at low tide went across on the stepping stones to Canvey, or at high tide by rowing boat.

About now I was starting my singing lessons with Miss Sally and progressing very well, according to her. She asked her uncle, the Padre, if I could sing a solo at the chapel next social hour. This was arranged and I was so nervous, but dear Miss Sally, who was playing for me, gave me a lovely smile. I thought, 'She's so kind I can't let her down,' so I sang 'My Task', a semi-religious piece. Fortunately everybody loved it, so I had to perform every Sunday.

This went on for a few months, then Sally suggested I enter for a Welsh Eisteddfod. I agreed, practised and went with her. To our amazement I got a Second-Class certificate. The adjudicator said, 'A lovely natural voice, should be trained.' Very nice, but some hopes! Rustling up a shilling a week for piano lessons was hard enough.

At the end of our street was an old warehouse, which was now being demolished. Two sisters, Miss Doris and Miss Muriel Lester, had bought the site. They then started having a beautiful building erected, called Kingsley Hall, in memory of their brother. It was to be a place of learning, worship and social activities for young and old. It was actually years before its time; now it would be called a Leisure Centre. When it was completed they gave a big tea party. It was lovely, all the Powis Road kids were there, me included.

I joined the library as I was a regular 'book worm', so my mother called me. In the course of time I became friends with Miss Muriel, who ran the library. She had noticed how much time I spent in there, so she asked if I would like to help her run it. I was delighted to do so.

Both Miss Muriel and Miss Doris, delightful ladies, were vegetarians. They wore no stockings, but sandals, and smock-like dresses and no make-up. I thought they were beautiful. Some people looked askance at them, but you could not help but like them, they were so kind and charming.

One evening my father said he had a surprise for us all. Tomorrow Vera and I were to hurry home from school and he was taking us all to the 'talking pictures'. This was almost unbelievable as we had only seen the silent screen about once, and other times the magic lantern at church socials. Off we went the next day to East Ham, a few stations past Bow. We joined a long queue of laughing people. After some time we were allowed in, bought our tickets and was ushered to our seats.

The lights dimmed, there was a sudden hush, and to our astonishment, up from the floor in front of the stage, like magic, came an organ, complete with a man playing. You could have heard a pin drop. Then a great roar of shouts and clapping began.

After a bit, the organ stopped and the picture came on the screen, the figures actually speaking. The film was *The Singing Fool* with Al Jolson. We were all enthralled. I've never forgotten that evening. We then went home to a high tea of winkles, shrimps and jelly with evaporated milk.

At school, which I loved, we had a very nice headmistress, Miss Drake, a charming, cultured lady who took rather a fancy to me and often took me to the theatre with her and her brother. I remember going to see *Through the Looking Glass* with them and having a lovely tea afterwards at a restaurant. A glimpse for me at a mode of life I now wanted for myself! She also took me to see the Beethoven Centenary Orchestra which had lots of violins in it. They moved me to pieces. I cried all the time; such a softie!

Lessons at school were a joy to me. I can remember one time the teacher was talking about the River Thames and where it started as a tiny stream and meandered through the countryside. I made a promise to myself that one day I would go and find where my beloved Thames started!

At home my father, who loved making things, had started to build a model boat: electric of course. After quite a while he finished it. I went with him one Sunday morning to the lake at Victoria Park, Hackney, to give it a trial run. It is so funny on looking back. My father showed me how to start the boat. Then he raced round to the other side before it crashed into the bank! Such excitement! He called the first boat he built 'Sparks'. It was a beautiful little craft about two feet long.

Other Sundays, as a change, we used to take a bus from Bow church to Gardeners' Corner, almost into the City. We would then go around finding historical buildings or plaques to famous people. In this way I learnt all about Old England, London in particular.

Some Sundays we used to go to Petticoat Lane. This was a noisy, jolly place, all kinds of things were sold there. Birds, dogs, crockery, cloth, etc. Very ribald remarks were made by the men selling. All the adults laughed but it went over my head. The language was very vulgar and suggestive, as I now realize.

As a treat some Sundays, Vera and I took it in turns to invite a friend to tea. This was great fun. In those days we had men who came round with a board on their heads selling muffins, another with a wheelbarrow selling shrimps, winkles and other delicacies! We loved having winkles, picking them out with a pin, and decorating the sides of our plates with the round black heads. Also we had jelly with evaporated milk poured over it. Such a treat!

By now Miss Muriel was inviting me to tea, and there I met several of her friends, very cultured people from whom I began to learn to speak better, and also hear about books and foreign countries. I was invited to the Christmas celebrations at Kingsley Hall to help with the parties Miss Muriel and her sister had planned for all and sundry. Afterwards I joined her at her own party. Here were several coloured people: some from

India, Jamaica and others from Germany, France and America. Most of what was said went over my head. I was very fascinated by the various national costumes some wore.

On 20 January 1927 my brother Arthur was born. I had always longed for a brother and I worshipped him from the start. I used to dash home from school to bathe him, feed him, play with him and rock him to sleep. All his life we were very close.

In April my father, for my 13th birthday, had saved up and bought me a second-hand piano to compensate for me not to have been able to do any sports. I had always been interested in music, so he arranged for me to have lessons to learn how to play. I was so very pleased; I couldn't start soon enough.

My mother's brother, Uncle John, had a toy shop and gave me a beautiful blonde doll with eyes that opened and closed, which was also double jointed! I couldn't believe it, she was so lovely. I immediately began to beg pieces of material from an aunt who made dresses for Vera and me. With these I made some fabulous frocks for my dolls: dreadfully sewn together, as I hated sewing, but rather good styles.

The next month, 8 May, was my mother's birthday. As I only had sixpence a week pocket-money I could not afford an expensive present. So, having saved ninepence for a present, I went off to the market in Roman Road, Old Ford. Here were many stalls selling everything you could think of. All hustle and bustle, the barrow boys in their glory shouting their wares with many a quip and saucy remark. All was very jolly but I was nervous being alone. I went round and round the stalls deliberating on what to buy. I had noticed a necklace on one stall, and had stood and admired it, asking the price. Ninepence I was told. After several askings the woman stall holder said, 'Take the "B" thing for sixpence or I'll never sleep tonight, those eyes will haunt me!' I quickly put down the six pennies and fled with the treasure.

At church now, I was singing in the choir, and sometimes as a soloist at the social meetings on Sunday nights. Learning to play the piano was helping my singing as I could play to practise scales.

Meanwhile, my father was still enthralled with his plots of land, but had now laid the foundation of the bungalow. He was working most evenings on making a tent for us all to sleep in on Canvey. He was planning for us all to spend a holiday there this year. The tent was terrific: run and fell seams hand-sewn with waxed thread. The span roof was to be supported by a centre pole. He made an excellent job of it.

Each summer before, we had always gone to Ramsgate for two weeks in the school summer holidays. It was, for me, very exciting. We used to go from Tower Bridge by the *Golden Sovereign* boat. I loved the water although I wasn't allowed to swim. I used to love to go down in the engine room with my father and watch. They were paddle boats then. I remember once the sea was so rough we had to go ashore at Margate. I was so thrilled, it was so exciting.

However, to Canvey we were going. My father had already ordered from Holmes Bros., the timber for a shed to be delivered.

What excitement setting up the tent. After Mother had settled baby Arthur in a cot, my little sister and I were given the job of sorting out the pegs and handing them to my father to bang into the ground, after he had marked out the site. Of course everything we did was wrong, we were only stupid little girls!

After a lot of grumbling, sore fingers, aching backs and some cross words between Mum and Dad, the tent was erected, hurrah! We had a Primus stove and had picked up groceries and milk from the High Street.

After we had a meal, rather rough and ready, we again set off for Holmes Bros. and there bought palliasses and ground sheets. We also ordered a delivery of paraffin oil and methylated spirits for the Primus. We had to make another journey to pick up the kettle, pots and pans, etc.

For three days we lived in the tent. Thank goodness for fine weather. Dad had started on the shed. He had already made a plan, so knew exactly the length to cut the timber. Of course I had to be the mate. What a soul-destroying job; nothing I did was right, it was always my fault if something didn't fit.

The third day saw the finish, just the felt to go on top of the roof. The shed was for cooking, washing and eating in, leaving the tent solely for sleeping in. By the end of the first week we were all tidy but worn out.

One horrific item still remained. We had a water butt at one corner of the shed, but so far, having no rain that wasn't any help. To fetch water we had to go for a walk as far as Homes Bros., about fifteen minutes away, to buy water in cans, jugs or whatever, for halfpenny a time. Then it had to be carried all the way back! As one had to cross a very rickety old wooden bridge, and climb over a dyke, you can imagine how much water you had left when you reached base! It was always my father, Vera and I who were the water carriers. Life was much easier after a downpour of rain. At least we only needed to get our drinking water or chance boiling the rainwater, which we often did.

I was never happy with the toilet facilities at home, but here I was horrified. Dad built a small shed, and we had an 'Elsan' chemical lavatory which had to be emptied regularly. Dad dug a deep hole in a corner farthest away from the tent and eating hut. After a while we all got a bit blasé about it and chanted some song as Dad was 'burying the dead' as we called it!

It was all very nice for a holiday, but I was eager to get back to Powis Road to my piano in the parlour, with its plush couch and armchairs, aspidistra and a gramophone that was wound up by hand. It had an enormous trumpet. This gramophone had a wax cylinder on which you could make your own records. We often did this; they were a scream!

My father made his own radio crystal set complete with earphones. He and Mother used to sit there with the earphones on laughing away and making us kids sit silent otherwise they couldn't hear it!

For years we had only gas mantels for lighting, open fires with ovens for cooking. The laundry was done in the kitchen. Irons you heated on the fire for ironing. To clean carpets and to keep down the dust one used to sprinkle tea leaves on the carpet then brush with a stiff brush! The fireplace also had to be 'blackened' and the brass fire-irons cleaned. Never a dull moment in the house for wives in those days.

I am now fourteen years old and due to leave school. I was devastated, I did so love my school days and my headmistress. I was also smarting over the shock of being turned down by the Examiners of Trade School Scholarships.

I had passed the English, maths, art and needlework exams, but you had to pass a medical and I was turned down because of the heart valve trouble which had meant a quite a loss of schooling. So I had to leave at fourteen to earn a living.

I was allowed to have a few weeks' holiday before looking for a job, so I spent most of my time with Miss Muriel. This year she had started to invite me to her special parties as my speech and manners had greatly improved after mixing so much with her and her sister.

Muriel and Doris had a lovely apartment at the top of the building. These days you would call it a penthouse. To me it was sheer luxury! I began going to meals with them which was exciting and different as they were vegetarians. Here I met lots of exciting people; Indian Princesses, Princes and Professors.

One lunch I was invited to, Muriel introduced me to a small, skinny, almost bald Indian wrapped in a loin cloth and white sheet. His name was Mahatma Ghandi! He was a very gentle and nice man and I enjoyed talking to him. He stayed at the Hall for two weeks.

I remember seeing him on several occasions. He used to walk down the street early in the morning and talk to all the people he met. They used to call out, 'How are you Mr Gandhi?'

The sisters Muriel and Doris had tried to change me to a vegetarian but I came from a family, on my mother's side, of butchers: all her five brothers were butchers in Smithfield.

My holiday was over, I must look for a job. I had always dreamed of working in a shipping office plotting the passage of ships with little flags! What a hope.

My mother apparently fancied having a dressmaker in the family. In actual fact if she sewed a button on it fell off at the first fastening. So off we went to a place called Toynbee Hall on the Whitechapel Road, who dealt with jobs for school-leavers.

The only job on offer this particular morning was for an apprenticeship at the House of Norman Hartnell, dressmakers to Society! Off we set, my mother a tall, auburn-haired, rather forbidding Scot and me a brown-haired, brown-eyed, long-legged, shy child. To my mother's delight the staff manageress was a Scot. Of course I was sunk; they got on like a house on fire. Miss McDonald she was called.

My wage was nine shillings per week and she told me my duties as an apprentice. It was for three years and I had to start at 8.30 a.m. and sweep floors, pick up and clean the pins, dole them out to the work tables, dust all the surfaces, fill Madame Simone's pin-cushion she wore on her wrist and do the rounds of the work tables! There were eight tables altogether, each with a First Hand, two assistants and one improver. I had to make list of items they needed from the stockroom. These consisted of Silko to match materials, hooks and eyes [no zips in those days], buttons to be made from materials to match the dresses, horse hair, lead weights, skirt binding called 'lute', Petersham, 'Hartnell' name-tabs to be sewn in the garments.

Then the hour for Madame to arrive!

As soon as she came in I had to dash downstairs out into Bruton Mews to the Beax Arts Café for a jug of coffee for her. Hartnell's premises in those days was at number 10 Bruton Street in the West End. In later years he moved across to number 26, so the back of our workrooms looked onto the Mews where cars instead of horses are now housed!

I was so scared of Madame Simone I used to come up the stairs quickly and nearly always slopped her coffee on the tray. She invariably greeted me with a volley of French, which I couldn't understand, but her manner terrified me. How I got through the first week I do not know.

Another of my duties was one that pleased me. I often had to go to the salon to fetch a model dress. For this I had to take a cover to wrap over the dress. I had my first glimpse of the salon proper as the dressing rooms were off the side. All crystal chandeliers, gilt chairs that looked as if they would break if you sat in them, and beautiful green velvet curtains with carpet to match. It was like a palace to me. I couldn't wait to get home and tell my mother all about it. But, alas, before I could go home I had to put all the chairs on top of the tables in the workroom and sweep the floors, cover everything that had been left uncovered, sewing machines for instance. All this, a 48-hour week, for just nine shillings.

There were five workrooms at Hartnell's, three of which were dressmaking rooms with Madame Simone, Mademoiselles David and Charlmange in charge of each. There was an embroidery room run by Mrs Pritchard and a lingerie room run by the two Misses Luke, sisters. The store room was managed by Mrs Cornwall and her assistant Louise.

This room was a veritable Aladdin's Cave in my eyes. Beautiful fabrics, and I mean beautiful, specially woven in France for Norman Hartnell. All pure silk and silk velvets of delicate colours.

While waiting my turn at the stock room I met the other apprentices. The two I chummed up with were Phyllis and Alice. Phyllis lived in Stepney Green, Alice at Mile End. As I lived at Bow we agreed to walk at night together to Charing Cross station for the underground train.

Our usual mode of walking was thus; Stepney Green on the left, Mile End on the right and Bow Road in the middle.

The other two were very knowing Cockney kids. They clearly knew what life was all about, unlike me. I was innocent as a babe! Most children of fourteen years were, in the 1920s.

On our walk to Charing Cross station from Bruton Street we crossed Bond Street, then went along Cork Street. All the premises here were military or naval tailors. Over these shops were flats, with their doorways being in between the shops.

One night as we walked, we could see a rather portly gentleman emerge from a tailors and proceed in the same direction as us. A second or two after him came a very over-dressed 'lady' from a doorway! I thought she looked wonderful. Black satin suit, small hat with a veil, but to crown it all she had a silver fox fur slung over one shoulder. To my innocent eyes she looked like an actress. Later on I learned she was of doubtful character. This lady had now caught up with our portly gent and was talking to him. 'Coo,' said Alice from Mile End Road to Phyllis from Stepney Green. 'Did you see that? Come on kids, let's follow them.' Upon which they quickened their steps, pulling poor ignorant Bow Road after them!

We trailed the couple through the Burlington Arcade out into Piccadilly, eventually arriving at Piccadilly underground outside Swan and Edgar's large premises. Down the steps we almost fell, and onto the escalator. We could see our gentleman friend and his pursuer. All the time the lady was pulling his arm and trying to talk him into something, but he would have nothing to do with her. Now my two companions gave up, not with very good grace I can tell you.

After that we proceeded down the Haymarket along by St-Martin-in-the-Fields church, then down the hill of Villiers Street to Charing Cross underground. We had many more 'to-dos' like this but it was many years before I knew what kind of 'lady' she was.

I proceeded with my apprenticeship running errands, sweeping up etc., then one awful day the Second Hand, one lady below Madame Simone, said 'It's about time this youngster learnt how to sew.'

They gave me needle and thread and showed me how to neaten seams by over-sewing the edges. Quite small stitches they were, supposed to be anyway. Mine were very uneven, some large some small, not a pretty sight! Still, I kept trying.

I was then shown how to make shoulder clips. In every dress or blouse that was made, were sewn these lengths of ribbon-like material with a press stud on one end. They were sewn with the press stud to the neck of the garment, the other end to the armhole seam itself. These were designed to stop shoulder straps of undies falling down on to your arm.

Name-tabs were also sewn in every finished garment; 'Norman Hartnell' embroidered on to ribbon about two and a half inches long. I was kept very busy doing these simple tasks as well as my cleaning up and visits to the stockroom.

Then came one day when I was to be taught 'Fly-running'. Horrors! Hartnell had a nasty habit of designing beautiful dresses in chiffon with lots of pin-tucking on them. The tucks were an eighth of an inch deep and half an inch apart. We had to work with the thread still on the reel, as you must not have a join in the stitches. To fly-run we used a very fine needle, Straw's No. 9, long ones. I was given a piece of chiffon, needle and reel of cotton to practise with.

The actual stitch was made by doing a few running stitches, very tiny ones, not taking the needle out but pushing it along with the second finger on your right hand so the needle never comes out, until you have gone right across the material. Well, I struggled but I could hardly move the needle. I was soaking the piece of chiffon with my blood! No one had checked to see if I was wearing a thimble, I did not possess one, so we started again. That evening I went home, cried and begged my mother not to make me go back. Go back and learn was the answer to my plea. So back I went, learn I did.

I was elevated after my three years' apprenticeship to 'Improver' thence to junior assistant then assistant to 'Hand'. That wonderful accolade after all those years of, to me, drudgery! I hated every minute of sewing. I was, however, attending evening classes taking Design. I was shown to have quite a talent for designing clothes. Now this I adored. For this I put up with the ghastly sewing to reap the results of my sketches.

I began to make clothes for my mother's friends, the Misses Muriel and Doris Lester and their friends. Not because I liked the sewing but I was earning some money.

Dressmakers' wages were very poor in the thirties. The wages for a First Class hand was only three pounds fifteen shillings for a 48-hour week, so you can see I needed the extra money.

Life at home had gone on much the same. I still went on my walks on Sunday morning with my father. I used to buy material in Petticoat Lane, really beautiful fabrics. I had also learnt how to beat the stall holders down in price. I'll never know how I managed this! I used to pluck up all my courage to do it.

Chapter 2

By now I had begun to notice boys! I had a boyfriend who was a Boy Scout. He was 21 years old and I was 19. He used to take me to the Stratford Empire Theatre to see a variety show, buy me some chocolates and gave me a very chaste goodnight kiss. I soon got bored with him as he had no conversation at all. I know I was a chatterbox but he just used to look at me and not utter a word. His name was Wally [aptly called!]

At Kingsley Hall I had met someone else, Mike. He was much nicer, with more repartee. I used to enjoy going around with him. I am sorry to admit I was a flirt! I just loved the males.

Mike didn't last long; I met three more very nice fellows at Kingsley Hall. One was a lawyer whose mother had a beautiful estate in Cornwall. The next one was a money broker in the City. These men were much older than me so their conversations were very interesting.

They used to meet me from Hartnell's and we'd have a lovely meal and then go to the Odeon in Leicester Square, and then they would take me back to Bow in their cars. I had a gorgeous time!

With all the lovely clothes I was making for myself and also the very nice Bentleys and MG cars that came for me, I gained the nickname 'Countess' from my friends and neighbours. They all used to come to their front doors to see what I was wearing when these cars came for me.

I had a friend called Kathy, who lived next door to the Bryant and May match factory on the other side of Bow Road to me. One Sunday she asked me to tea with her and her mother. When I arrived there was also an elderly lady there. Naughty Kathy introduced me to this nice old lady as 'The Countess'. All flustered the dear soul dropped a curtsy and said, 'Pleased to meet you My Lady'. I felt awful but Kathy and her mother, tongue in cheek, carried on with the tea party. Later when I married I sent her a piece of wedding cake 'From The Countess'. Kathy said she showed it to all her old friends. I wonder if she ever ate it!

By now my father had finished his bungalow on Canvey Island. We used it some weekends and all holidays. I had got very friendly with one of the Holmes Bros. Builders Merchants on Canvey, Fred his name was. He had known me from the first time we went to Canvey. I felt very cheeky calling him Fred as he was sixteen years older than me. I had called at his shop for something and he asked me if I had seen the Southend lights. I said not really, only from Canvey, but they looked very good. He then said, 'Ask your father if I may take you to see them this evening'.

I dashed home very excited, asked Dad and he said OK, but I had to be home by ten o'clock. I went off to view Southend lights with Fred, excited but slightly apprehensive. I suppose it was being with a man instead of my usual boyfriends.

I went to meet Fred at the shop. After a while we set out in his lovely Lagonda car. We just purred along and I felt like a queen. I had been in cars before but they had all been Bentleys, Fords or little open sports. In those days there was no bridge at Canvey so you bumped over at low tides on stepping stones. You also had to watch the times of the tide to return or you had to leave your car and come out by rowing boat.

We arrived at Southend and, truly, it was marvellous. Down the centre of the promenade was about twenty feet or more of grass. In this grass was erected lots of glass flowers on tall stems, leaves as well. All had electric bulbs inside of them to light them up. It was truly fairy land. The flowers were bluebells, daisies and sunflowers, all absolutely magical. There was room enough each side of the grass to allow cars one side up and one side down. Of course it took ages to go along, it was really nose to bumper.

Fred took me to the Palace Hotel on the Front near the Pier, I thought for a coffee, but he ordered a gin and tonic for me and said he was sure I'd like it. I did, and did not let on it was the first time I'd had such a drink!

We then made our way back to Canvey. On top of Essex Way, which is a very steep hill, we stopped to admire the view. It was indeed impressive, all the lights on Canvey twinkling, and those back at Southend. We sat there for some time, then he pressed a switch and we heard *Lover come back to me* being sung on the radio. I loved that song. It was so romantic sitting there in the dusk listening.

Well, when that was finished we had to go or swim for it. I just about got home in time. It was a very nice evening but somehow I felt uneasy. Perhaps it was the age difference.

Back to work and the usual routine. About six of us girls went out in a group. We always had a good time. In my youth I was remarkably like Jessie Mathews the actress. Invariably one of the lads would come up and say, 'Hello Jessie, how about a dance?' It sort of broke the ice for my friends because the chums of my partner would dance with them also.

As it was September all the dances would begin, so I began to design some pretty dresses to wear. The first evening out was a police ball held at a hall on the Mile End Road, and I went with my usual friends. Once more a boy came up and said, 'Hello Jessie, may I have this dance?' I looked at him and thought, *Oh yes please*, but calmly said, 'Yes'. His name was David. He was the same height as me with dark brown eyes and hair, a roguish face and cheeky smile. He had it all. Oh how I loved him, I had fallen in love at first sight! He had four friends with him and they paired with my friends which included my younger sister Vera. From then on we were a group. We got permission from my father to go to Canvey for a weekend, on condition the tent was put up for the boys' sleeping accommodation. Us girls could sleep in the bungalow. All these things were attended to.

We began a lovely weekend, five lads and five girls. After a day on the beach then home for a good meal, we sat around a bonfire singing all kinds of songs [some naughty, some nice], a little kissing and hugging in the light of the fire and so to bed. Girls in the room, boys in the tent. Each day and night a repetition of before. We all left for home having had a wonderful time. Could that happen today? Your guess, dear reader, is as good as mine.

This was the first of many weekends. At this period I joined a club called the Comrades Circle run by the London Co-operative Society. No politics just a social and educational club. I studied local government and economics. I was made secretary of the social side. At our socials and dances I often sang at the piano, by now having a very good mezzo soprano voice.

One evening, as I recall, one of the girls had been very nasty to me over something and while I was singing she and her boyfriend were sitting quite near the piano. So the next song I sang was directed at her boyfriend. It was called 'I've never had a lesson in my life, but I know just how to make love'. I had him squirming in his seat! His girlfriend was furious because during the rest of the evening he was hanging around me! I didn't want him, it was just to punish her. She was never rude to me again.

The economics lecturer was a dish and after three weeks was dating me. Professor Arthur Jupp was his name. I very nearly failed the exam as I had been out late the night before with him. Luckily I managed to scrape through.

I still belonged to the Social Club, and as Secretary had arranged for a weekend away. I had booked a hotel for twenty of us at Torquay, a lovely seaside resort. We had arrived, and after lunch all went for a walk along the seafront. Someone said, 'Wouldn't it be nice to have a boat trip? How about it, Billie, could you arrange it for us?' I said, 'Why me? I don't know if they have boat trips at this snooty place. Anyway I'll try.'

So we made our way along the quay when I saw two men in a small boat. I shouted 'Ahoy there! Do you do boat trips?' The two men looked at each other, mumbled something, then the younger of the two shouted, 'Half a minute we'll come ashore.' This they did and I told them what we wanted and that there were twelve of us. 'OK,' he said. 'Tomorrow morning at 9.30 a.m.' I thanked them and told my friends.

We duly presented ourselves the next morning and to our amazement it was a beautiful big yacht! It was a picture. The two fellows helped us aboard and the elder one said to me, 'I've got oilskins for you.' He then took me down into a cabin and proceed to garb me out with a sou'wester and yellow oilskin coat. This was enormous on me. We then went on deck and one of my friends said, 'Hi skipper' jokingly.

We had a whale of a time. I love the water, it was quite choppy. I was with 'Dennis', as he told me to call him, at the helm. We were soaked by spray. It was so exhilarating, I thoroughly enjoyed myself.

We had by now returned to the quay. All the others had got off the boat and I stayed to ask how much we owed them. The young man said, 'You'll have to ask Dennis, it's his boat.' Rather shaken I approached Dennis and on asking he said, 'Nothing, I've thoroughly enjoyed having you.'

'But,' said I, 'you should have told us you didn't do trips.'

'My pleasure,' he said, laughing.

After thanking him he said, 'Hold on, you're not going yet are you?' I said 'Of course I am, it's my party, I'm in charge.'

'Well have dinner with me then will you?' I told him that I would and he arranged to pick me up at the hotel at 7 p.m. that evening.

When I went back to the group they were astounded at not having to pay.

'We'll always send you, Billie, to get us such a treat,' someone said!

Dennis picked me up and took me to The Grand, I think, a beautiful hotel. He told me about himself and said that he had a sister he would like me to meet, and said, 'Must you go home tomorrow? We could sail up the River Dart, you'll love it.' We had a wonderful evening. If only I could have stayed over.

We exchanged addresses, promising to keep in touch. We left at 11 a.m. the next morning. I never saw him again. It was a pleasant interlude however. It's now 1935, the Silver Jubilee of King George and Queen Mary. Our street held a big party for all the children. I'm happy to say I did a lot of cake-making as I loved cooking. We all dressed up and wore paper hats, sang God Save The King, and also Merry England. A wonderful day. I've always been very patriotic.

I used to go along to the Co-op's Tennis Club in Stratford with my Professor Arthur. I never played; too energetic for my ticker. There I met Sonny, a tea planter from India on his six month's leave. He and Arthur vied with each other for my company. I had a whale of a time with all the dinners and shows.

I'll always remember coming to Leigh-on-Sea with Sonny to view some lovely houses being built on the cliff top. On the way to Leigh from London, Sonny asked me if we saw a house I like, would I marry him. Well I didn't want to marry anyone, I was enjoying life too much. Anyway, when we saw the house, one was so beautiful, complete with sunken bath, I nearly said I would marry him! But common sense ruled the day; I never said yes.

Back at Hartnell's I happened to be working on a gown for Ascot for a client. I could not get the dress done until 10 o'clock on the day my client, Mrs Woolf, wanted it. So I went into the workroom very early to finish on time. There was a certain something on the dress I wasn't sure of, so I took the wrapper to the salon to look at the model. This must have been about 8 o'clock so no one was about, the cleaners had gone too. I took two steps into the salon, this beautiful room before me. I just started to walk down the room as I had seen the model girls do, dragging the wrapper behind me as if it were my mink! Oh, it was fantastic, I could see myself in the mirrors round the room. I'd certainly forgotten my rush order, just revelling in the beauty around me, when someone coughed! Oh God, I recognized that cough; Hartnell's!

I turned around, wishing the floor would swallow me up, when he said, 'Who taught you to walk like that?' I shrugged my shoulders and said, 'No one, I just walk.' He replied, 'How would you like to work in the salon?' Now I was twenty and my answer was, 'I would love to but I'll have to ask my mother.'

'You do that and let me know what she says,' he replied.

Well I had a quick look at the model I'd come to check and dashed back to the workroom on wings! That day was the longest I'd ever known. Eventually I arrived home, but trying to work out how I was going to put the question to my mother. I worded the question as if I was going to be an assistant in the salon, not a model girl who had to paint her face! I managed to put the question and, as I thought she would, she said, 'What about your dressmaking?' Well I said that I was fully qualified now and could never forget what I'd learnt, this was a new venture.

After talking it over with my father, he agreed as I knew he would. I could go into the salon as Mr Hartnell suggested.

The next day back at work I kept looking at the time. Mr Hartnell's normal arrival time was 10 o'clock. So, ten past ten I excused myself, not to go where everybody thought I was going, but to Hartnell's office. In I walked, but as I looked at him expecting him to recognize me, he looked blankly at me. *Gosh*, I thought, *he's forgotten all he said*. Hesitantly, I started to remind him, he then recovered himself to say 'Oh yes, I'll ring Madame Eileen to fix a time for you to see her.' This he did and she said that I could start in two weeks' time.

It wasn't what I'd hoped for but it was something. But, unbeknown to me, fate was working for me.

We made clothes for lots of actresses including Anny Ahlers, an Austrian actress, who was ordering clothes for her new show. She had already chosen the clothes and had one fitting, but unfortunately had to go to America. In those days you never flew Concorde, it took ages to get there and back, you usually went by sea. Unfortunately, something had to be done. Madame Simone looked at me and then measured me, and by a stroke of luck I was the exact size and similar in all respect as Anny Ahlers [except for her glorious long auburn hair and beauty].

So I was called several times a day in to the fitting rooms to have her costume fitting on me. There were many costumes being made, so I was hardly in the workroom. Madame Simone said I'd better go up there to the salon and stay!

I was over the moon, just what I wanted. I couldn't get home quickly enough to tell Mother. I was going to have an increase in salary. Also a green satin dress made for me the same as all the salon staff had. Of course I did not model or even learn straight away. I had certain duties in the salon every day.

After about six weeks Madame Eileen then showed me how to walk and turn nicely. To do this I had to balance heavy books on my head [at least to me they were heavy] and not let them fall off! Quite hard to do really. I practised this at home and in a very short time mastered it.

Another trick I had to learn was how to turn around when wearing a dress with a train, i.e. either a wedding dress or a debutante's coming-out gown! After a lot of practice I got it right.

I began by showing simple afternoon dresses to clients under supervision of Madame Eileen, or one of the other model girls. Hartnell always in those days had four house models. For his shows twice a year at Grosvenor House, Park Lane, he would have extra freelance models.

Life proceeded to be very exciting at work and at home. I was making myself extra-special clothes to wear, learning to make up my face and having my long curly hair styled at a very smart hairdresser's in Dover Street. All my friends hardly knew me!

One lovely perk of the job was that we models were often invited to society weddings at St Margaret's at Westminster, with the receptions held at Claridges. One such wedding I went to was Miss Oonagh Guinness. The bride wore a marvellous cream satin gown embroidered in gold. She carried a sheaf of golden corn. There were six bridesmaids in the palest pink to deepest pink. They each had male attendants. Each pew where the bridesmaids stood was decorated in the same colour as her dress. It was wonderful. I'd never seen anything so beautiful.

Another nice perk was the actresses we made gowns for, used to give us theatre tickets. I provided most of my friends with them. We made fabulous dresses for Lilly Elsie, Evelyn Laye, Beatrice Lilly and Binnie Barnes. While all this was happening at Hartnell's my social life had also changed. I was no longer helping to run the library at Kingsley Hall, but became more of a companion to Muriel Lester. Some weekends she would take me to Leatherhead in Surrey to visit her friend Mr Percival Weaver, a very wealthy business man.

He had a lovely big old manor house standing in acres of woodland. In one part of the wood he'd had a clearance made and erected charming wooden chalets. These he used as guest houses for all his international friends. Muriel and I would stay in the main house. The only snag for me was that they were all vegetarians. I, alas, adored MEAT! But I did not mind just for the weekend. Actually I rather liked some of the food.

While at Leatherhead I met Professor Edmond Szekely from Montego Bay, Jamaica, who was director of the International Cosmotherapeutic

Expedition 1930 to 1940. He was most charming and had a beautiful speaking voice. I spent many a pleasant hour with him talking about England, our cultures, habits, etc. and the differences of his country. I also met Diana Cripps, daughter of Sir Stafford Cripps, another charming person.

In between my visits to Leatherhead I spent many pleasant hours with my various boyfriends, although I must admit I was seeing an awful lot of David.

Most of our little band had broken up and had gone their separate ways. We all exchanged Christmas cards for years to come. Bill had unfortunately died and Jeff had joined the Mounted police in Canada. The girls had also their particular boyfriends.

On the odd occasion I went to Canvey, I still saw Fred Holmes and perhaps had a meal with him. All very nice, in the meantime we exchanged letters now and again, so kept each other *au fait* of our goings on!

Unfortunately I went down with rheumatic fever and in those days you were confined to bed, soaked with Wintergreen oils and wrapped in a blanket. The doctor gave medicine, I don't remember what.

It was nine whole months before I was passed fit enough for work again. I soon regained my spirits [we Cockneys are hard to suppress] and found my position at Hartnell's was obviously filled.

I was lucky enough to get a model's job. I didn't want to sew again, only for myself. This job was at Madame Hermines in Bond Street on the opposite corner to 'Aspreys'.

Having been back at work for a while I found my heart was not as good as it was before; I had to slow down a lot, which did not suit me! I would have a go at most things, good or bad for me. I really enjoyed working at Hermine's; they made a great fuss of me as I had been at Hartnell's!

Madame and her husband, the Baron De Garda, used to invite me for dinner their home in Knightsbridge. I would then be taken to the station in their chauffeur-driven car! It was whilst I was there I met Amy Johnson, the first woman to fly the Atlantic Ocean. As a matter of fact Hermine's made her wedding garments – wait for it – it was a black suit, big black hat and white blouse! Apparently black was Jim Mallison's favourite colour, Jim being the husband-to-be!

I was invited to the wedding. They were married at St George's, Hanover Square. She was always my heroine from then on. Some day I promised myself I would fly a plane! Some hopes!

During this time I was seeing a lot of David. Going steady, I think they call it today. David had suggested we go on holiday together to a Holiday Camp, a new venture started by Billy Butlin. I would have loved to have gone but my parents would not give permission. In any case the moral standards of the day frowned on this kind of thing. Actually these camps were lots of chalets set in large grounds with a main hall for dining and leisure pursuits. You can imagine the goings on of certain members of the public.

After this refusal of mine he did not seem so keen. Later in the year I arranged a get-together of our little crowd, including David, at our bungalow on Canvey at Easter 1937. Conditions as before, boys in the tent, girls in the bungalow. All seemed set but David asked if he could bring someone he'd met at Butlins. I said yes, thinking it was another boy. We had all arrived on Canvey and to my surprise David's friend was a girl. I covered up my embarrassment and assigned a bed for her. It meant me sharing with someone. The first day went like any other. The evening after dinner, the usual sing-song around the bonfire went merrily on until bedtime. We girls all turned into the bungalow, after chatting a bit I learnt the new girl's name was Mary and that she had met David at Butlins and was, as far as I gathered, considering herself his girlfriend. I just couldn't believe it. I went to sleep crying softly to myself.

In the morning I woke early to make tea and found the place allotted to Mary empty. After breakfast when we were washing up in the kitchen she told Peggy, my sister's friend, that she had slept with David that night! Of course, Peggy told me. I was so upset, also angry, at being treated this way.

I left the bungalow and walked to the village to find a telephone. I then proceeded to ring Fred Holmes who lived in Westcliff-on-Sea, telling him I was in a spot and needed to be rescued. He was surprised but rose to the occasion. It could not be until one hour's time as the tide was still in. Eventually, having packed my bag, given my sister Vera the keys for the bungalow, I walked out telling David why I was going. I never saw him again! I did love that boy and wept many a tear for him.

Fred drove me to his parents' home in Westcliff; his mother very kindly invited me for the rest of the weekend. I told Fred all the miserable story and wept on his shoulder. He was very kind but not very demonstrative which was good for the moment.

I went on working, this time not so happy and carefree. I did feel most hurt over David and did not realize how much I loved him. His parents, who I also liked a lot, wrote and said how sorry they were to lose me and had been looking forward to having me in the family.

Around this time I was seeing more of Fred, as I was going to Canvey most weekends with a girlfriend. Fred came up to Bow several times to take me out. Very charming, not wanting to maul me like some of the other boyfriends. To be honest I was rather sick of having to fight for my honour every time a man took me out! To be with Fred he at least never annoyed me with all that. Naïve would you say? Perhaps it was just balm to my senses to be treated with just kindness at the moment.

The month of August had come around again. This year I decided to go on a holiday with a friend from work, Christine. We went for a week to Bournemouth. For the second week I joined my parents at the bungalow on Canvey, seeing Fred almost every evening.

Back to work again, and the usual rounds of making new winter clothes. At the end of September I had a weekend on Canvey with my sister Vera, and her friend Peggy.

On the Saturday afternoon I went for a drive with Fred, going back to his home in Westcliff to water the plants in the conservatory. While doing this Fred, very matter of factly, asked me to marry him! All I could think of saying, very stupidly, was, 'But I haven't got any money.' He said, 'No matter I've enough for two.'

He opened a bottle of wine from his father's cellar, we toasted each other, the die was cast!

When I got back to the bungalow I couldn't tell my sister. I think I was in a state of shock. Oh my God, I had to tell my parents who I knew were not very gone on Fred. When I did tell them my father roared, 'He's too damned old for you by sixteen years, he's had many affairs and is too mature.'

Apparently Fred and his brother had quite a reputation, which I of course didn't know. What did I care, he was kind to me, I've promised him now and I want to be married.

Next day at the salon I told my fellow models the news. When? What will you wear? Questions were shot at me. Naturally I hadn't considered these things at the moment.

The next weekend I went to Westcliff to stay with Fred's parents. We talked about the date of the wedding. We wanted to find a house or a bungalow before I'd set a date. So, we started that very morning. From the estate agents we got several properties to look at in Leigh, Westcliff and surrounding villages.

In Leigh we found a very nice bungalow in Barnard Road. The people who owned it were not moving out until November. We paid a deposit there and then so as not to lose it. We could see that although structurally it was good, there would be quite a lot we could improve on.

So, we decided we would get married in January 1939. In those days girls used to have a bottom drawer where you collected bed and house linen 'hopefully'. Also there was a dress to be considered.

To my dismay, Fred refused to marry in a church; now I should have realized something here, also the fact there was no engagement ring! Being me I gave in and settled for a Register Office in Southend.

On behalf of my parents I booked a reception at the Poplar Road House Restaurant, Leigh, which in my day was a very nice place indeed. With all that settled, there was still the dress.

I hid away the design of a lovely white wedding dress I had designed for the day I married. Instead, I did a rather beautiful design of a blue chiffon with a hand-ruched bodice. One of the men who brought material from France, who I knew, made a present of a beautiful velvet hat to match the blue of my dress, and pair of long suede gloves also dyed to match. They were exquisite.

My shoes were also blue, and I was going to have a spray of pale pink carnations. My sister was to wear a deeper blue dress. All very nice but I wept a few tears for my white church wedding. Having been brought up with a chapel background, another black mark in my father's view for Fred.

We at Powis Road had also been thinking of moving. Dad found a nice house in Poplar, which had a spare bedroom that we could make into a bathroom of sorts. We moved in just before Christmas 1938. My sister and I still sharing a bedroom, my brother in one and Mum and Dad in the other. The reason for us moving was that my mother's mother was getting old and infirm and needed to live with us. She was going to have a bed-sitting room on the ground floor.

The layout of the ground floor was as follows: Quite a wide hall and just inside from the front door was the door to the parlour, a lovely big room with bay windows to the front. Beyond that, the door to my gran's room. Opposite her door were the stairs. Going on down the hall was the dining room, at the back was the kitchen.

Now on New Year's Eve my parents were out visiting, brother and sister also out, leaving just Gran and me. I had been invited out but my father said, 'You are going to be married on the 14th January; you shouldn't go out with the others.' So here I was, feeling bad tempered and thwarted. I thought I'd do some ironing and have the wireless on, and then have a rest and perhaps a coffee; 'Camp' in those days.

I'd just put the iron back on the fire and looked up, seeing right down the hall to Gran's door, when to my amazement I saw Gran come out and start to go up the stairs. 'Hey Gran, what do you want? I'll get it for you,' shouts I. To my astonishment she still kept going.

I put down the dress I was ironing and quickly went up the hall to the stairs, noticing that Gran's door was shut. Gran had never gone upstairs since she had been with us. I looked up the stairs, no one. Dashed up and looked into all the rooms, all empty!

Down I came and went into Gran's room without knocking. I was beginning to feel worried, but there was Gran sitting at her table quietly sewing; she did beautiful patchwork.

'Gran, did you go upstairs?' I asked as calmly as I could.

'No dear,' said Gran, 'did you want me?'

'No-oo,' I said and withdrew and went back to the dining room, sitting down to collect myself. The old lady I saw was dressed in the same kind of clothes Gran wore! Her hair was drawn back into a bun, with a little lace cap on top. I kept hoping my parents would soon come home as I did not want to go upstairs to bed on my own! I have never told anyone about this; they'd say I had imagined it.

Each weekend, although being winter and the weather being pretty bad, I'd go to Leigh with Fred and work on the bungalow getting it ready for 14 January. It was very hard work, something I had never done before. Rubbing paint down with sandpaper, scraping old wallpaper off the walls! My poor hands.

During the week I sewed on my trousseaux. On Friday 13 January I went to Leigh to stay at Fred's brother's house. The next morning, 14 January 1939, I awoke to a day that was so far away from the days of my dreams. My people arrived from Poplar and were at the Holmes' residence at Westcliff.

We all met at the Register Office in the London Road, Southend, a drab and musty building, no flowers. We all assembled in this unfriendly room with rows of chairs in front of a long table. A tall, unfriendly-looking man proceeded with the marriage service, if you could call it that.

I don't think I quite took it all in until we were leaving. Someone threw confetti and I had a ring on my finger. I was married!

I must be honest, and say I did not love Fred but was very fond of him, and in a strange way was sorry for him and wanted to take care of him. Strange and unusual thoughts to have on your wedding day!

We all went to the Poplar Road House Restaurant at Leigh for a very nice reception. Fred and I left in his Lagonda for our bungalow in Barnard Road, Leigh. On arriving at the bungalow, we found the woman we had engaged to light fires and get the place ready for us. Before doing anything else, I changed my clothes and went shopping in London Road, Leigh, for the Sunday dinner [so romantic].

In the butcher's shop I was still excited, I had to tell someone, so to a woman beside me I said, 'I've just got married.' She said, 'Oh my goodness, where do you live?' I told her, and she replied that she lived a few houses away.

Fred and I settled down and had quite a nice evening together. We listened to the radio [no television then] and played the gramophone. After a while I was tired, and went to get ready for bed feeling rather embarrassed. I got into the pretty nightie I'd had made for this very night. I lay in bed for quite a while before Fred came in. He promptly put out the light, got into bed, kissed me 'goodnight' and turned over away from me.

I just couldn't believe it. At least I expected to be cuddled, not ignored like this. Little did I know that life was going to be like this for the next forty-eight years. If I did I would have run away then. The bungalow we had brought was very nice. It had a large sitting room which looked on to a very pretty garden. At the end were fruit trees and a vegetable plot. The rest was lawn and flower beds. To have a garden and kitchen of my own was bliss. Life went on with no more affection than a chaste goodnight kiss, almost like brother and sister.

During the summer months, the tension in Germany was growing. This man Hitler was doing terrible things! We all felt something should be done. Then he overstepped himself. He invaded poor little Poland. This was after signing a pact with Mr Chamberlain, the British Prime Minister!

Now it's War! We had had enough. We all went mad making black-out curtains for windows. Stocking up on food, if you could afford it of course. After a bit we had several air raids. German bombers began to come over the Channel.

Living at the top of Leigh Cliffs we were able to see them coming in the distance. We could also see in the daylight of course our gallant boys of the Royal Air Force going out to meet them. Oh, those brave Spitfire fighters. Many a dog-fight, and alas many Spitfires were shot down. Some Germans got through to London where they did dreadful damage to life and buildings.

Later on, all the men here in Leigh who were too old to be called up, got together and formed a 'Home Guard'. My husband, who had been in the Royal Flying Corps in the First World War, was put in charge of one of the groups. These groups are subject of mirth these days, but believe me they were great. It's no joke when you're middle-aged to be on guard all night in winter, especially after doing a day's work.

Soon we were rationed with food. Coupons were issued for clothes, sweets, tinned food if you could get it. As for fruit, there were no oranges or bananas, none of the fruit from abroad. Everything became very scarce. Practically everyone had an air-raid shelter either indoors or out. We had an Anderson shelter in the garden, but we seldom used it. Everything was wet and horrible. When the raids were really bad we would dash across the road, to what used to be an allotment, but was now a shelter with benches along each side, a ghastly place. Everybody went down there when the sirens sounded. Sometimes the raid would last for hours, coming out only at the 'All Clear'. Not this lady! To my husband's disgust I would be standing on top of the shelter cheering our boys on as they tried to stop them getting through our barrage on their deadly way to London. I never realized how bloodthirsty I was until I heard myself yelling 'Kill 'em'. If only I had been a man I would have been up there with them!

Another drawback to the shelter was the makeshift toilet down there. Behind a tarpaulin cover, just a couple of buckets! When anybody went behind the screen we all sing 'Tipperary' the song from World War One.

When we first bought the bungalow we had some alterations made. We had the large loft upstairs made into a very nice spare bedroom and workroom for me, also this meant a staircase. It was one night, when sitting on the stairs during an air raid counting the minutes between the falling bombs, it seemed as if the next would be ours. We held our breath, and for the first time ever, sat with our arms around each other! To our amazement nothing happened, we could still hear the plane. Then all at once there was an almighty bang and our windows in the front room had blown out – slates and chimney blown off! Soot came down the chimney into our rooms. We could not believe it. Apparently the next bomb had fallen a short distance away on a church and also several houses killing a man. Were we lucky! There was an amazing incident one day when Fred and I were sitting on the stairs when the Germans were dropping parachute bombs. These sailed down just making a swishing sound, which we got to recognize. Well, we were just sitting quietly when we heard this peculiar noise which sounded as if it was coming from a big Poplar tree in our front garden. After a few minutes we thought we'd check what it was and got ready to run. We went out on to the path and there it was – a hedgehog coming along the path, his claws making the familiar swishing noise! Laugh, we nearly had hysterics!

Each week we had to go further afield to find a shop open. By this time the police had been round to every house asking people if possible to leave the town. We had to take the distributor arms from our cars and take them to the main police headquarters in Southend. All the beaches had barbed wire and cement blocks on them to stop an invasion. No lights were allowed to show either.

One particular morning I went with my sister-in-law to find a shop open. We were walking along the Cliffs at Leigh when we heard, then saw, a German plane coming towards us. We couldn't believe how low he was. To our horror he started to machine-gun us! We ran like mad until we came to a chemist shop at the top of Leigh Hill. Fortunately it had a deep doorway. In we dived, baskets and handbags flying! We saw the bullets go past the door. Phew! We sat there stunned, then both burst into tears. My husband and his brother were also machine-gunned early one evening coming up the Cliffs from the station.

After the police warning, those that could left the town. We couldn't go as my husband was doing work for the military who were stationed on Canvey Island. Not having the car, he now bought a bike. What a come-down for him, from a Lagonda car to a bike.

There were just two other couples left in our road now. Our friends the 'Cherrys' and the dairyman and his family. In the road opposite there was a family called West. Mr and Mrs West had two sons at sea and a daughter at school. Other friends of mine who hadn't left were solitary occupants in their roads. Even under these trying times we managed to have little get-togethers. We made cakes with dried egg, a small amount of a precious sugar ration, and mixing mashed potato into the butter – also carrots!

Surprisingly they were quite good. It was quite something to put a meal on the table seven days a week with just a few ounces of meat. We made nut rissoles, vegetable rissoles, the mind boggles! My greatest culinary achievement was when my sister Vera got married. I had her reception at my bungalow with twenty-seven guests. I went to the Food Office to beg, and almost made love to the official who interviewed me! Proudly I came home with quite a bunch of coupons.

Chapter 3

It is now 1941, and I had been married for two years and our marital relations had improved slightly. I think he made love to me about once a month. I never enjoyed this at all as he totally ignored my feelings, just satisfied himself and left me almost screaming with frustration!

I had begun to notice, on the rare occasion of our union, he would go into the dining room to his desk. I knew that's what he was doing because the pull-down top squeaked when let down. After noticing this several times I thought I would investigate when he was out, and see if I could find the purpose of his visits. I looked into the pigeon-holes, then a small drawer in the middle. Ah-ha, here is something. In the envelope was a condom. Why? I asked myself, there's no need for this, I dearly wanted a child. So, I got a thick darning needle and pierced the damned thing all over, but as I drew the needle out the rubber went together again. So I did this several times, hoping some damage was done!

When Fred and I moved into the bungalow, everybody in the road thought we were father and daughter. Well he was sixteen years older than me, and I looked young for my age. Mrs West thought I would be a nice girl for one of her sons. She began to invite me for coffee when each lad was on leave. It happened that the next time both were home together, I had realized what Mrs West had in mind, so, cheeky me, when I went to coffee to meet the lads I removed my wedding ring. Just for a lark! I had a very jolly time flirting outrageously with both lads. They vied with each other to take me for walks in Belfairs Wood. Although the woods had barbed wire, cement blocks and gun emplacements, one could walk through the golf course. One time they were arguing about who was taking me, when I suggested Gladys, the sister, came as well. You should have seen their faces!

However, off we went, had a lovely walk, it's very pretty there, and we were just coming out of the woods, when out of the sky came the Huns who started to blaze away at us. We all fell to the ground and wriggled into a ditch. Happily none of us were hurt but very, very scared. A very subdued foursome returned home.

Pete, the younger of the boys, had really got it bad about me, and I thought it was about time to own up to my relationship with my husband. Ken took it very well, but poor darling Pete wouldn't believe it. I was very ashamed, but his mother said she was glad that his first love was a nice girl like me!

My sister's husband, George, was in the Royal Air Force and stationed for a time at Winchester. He was due to go overseas at any moment, and they invited me to visit for a long weekend. I did just that and had a whale of a time. George was in the Medical Corps, as in 'civvy street' he was a Pathologist. After some time, he was sent to Burma to study the diseases the men in the jungle were going down with.

In our road we began to have convoys of Army lorries. Quite a few of them were Canadians who parked here. These were a jolly lot of men, miles from home, so the few of us began to let them have baths, or let them come in for the evenings just to make them feel at home. They were grand lads, so very grateful for our friendship. They showed us pictures of their families. When it was time for them to move on we cried and so did they. I wonder how many survived? We all prayed for them, we had all been such friends.

One of the most heart-rending scenes I can remember was seeing a contingent of Polish airmen, pilots and crews, marching through Leigh to Southend. Most of these had been rescued from the sea, having been shot down by the German planes. Nearly all were bandaged, their faces with torment written across them, and their tattered clothes brought tears to our eyes. These brave Polish lads were going to join our Air Force to fight on. They were in Southend for some while getting fit enough for duty again. Our little group all got together to give them hospitality. We all knitted like mad for them; socks, mittens, balaclava helmets, etc. Those poor brave souls, I wanted to hug them all.

It was Christmas again in a few weeks but Hitler was giving London hell. My parents lived in Poplar, quite near the docks, and these seemed to be Hitler's aim at the moment to destroy them. Night after night we heard the bombers going over up to London. I used to pray my dear parents were safe. After one terrible night I could stand it no longer. I caught a train, one of the few still running to Barking. From there I hitched a ride on a Brewery cart. The driver couldn't believe I wanted to go to Poplar. 'My God, woman, it's all on fire,' he said. 'Well my mum and dad are there so I've got to go,' said I.

When he put me down near the Blackwall Tunnel I couldn't recognize the place. Where on earth had Dunkheld Street gone? I very gingerly made my way through the rubble, burnt timber and smashed furniture, to a group of black-faced people rooting through the rubble. *Oh God no*, I thought, *where are they?* Near a makeshift shed over a brazier, someone was dispensing tea. I made for this and someone told me where my parents were, and that they were alive and well, although terribly shocked. I immediately got in touch with the Wardens in the district, left my address and particulars with them, and took my parents back with me. Off we went, blackened and rather bedraggled by now, arriving home to the surprise of my husband.

Fred got onto an estate agent friend of his to see if there were any houses or bungalows nearby we could possibly rent. We found a bungalow in Vardon Drive, about seven minutes' walk from us. That night Mum and Dad slept on the three-seat settee and a camp bed.

The next morning, after Fred had gone to business, I scoured the town for second-hand furniture. The bungalow had some bits and pieces left in it, thank goodness. I then went armed with brush-pan, duster, brooms, etc., to clean up. Fortunately I had enough bed linen to loan them for the time being. They moved in not having much luggage anyway and settled down very quickly, I was glad to see. Dad started tidying up the garden. Fortunately the people who owned the bungalow had left all the gardening tools. I took Mum around shopping for whatever we could get and so we settled down a bit. When all the London children had been evacuated to the country, my young brother Arthur was sent to Oxford to stay with Sir and Lady Iveah. A marvellous house, the kindest of people.

Later on in the summer, Mother said she'd like Arthur to come home for a short visit. He was about twelve years old then, a very sensible capable boy. Well, he came, and on the second night of his stay we had a dreadful raid. I think what must have happened was London was so heavily guarded and protected, that the German bombers couldn't get in to drop their bombs. So, they dropped them all here on the coast! We had fires everywhere.

Then, would you believe it, my mother was bombed again. Hers was the first whole house to remain standing. Windows and doors blown out of course but the building was intact! Round to our bungalow they came covered in soot. You would never believe it but my brother and father had their trouser pockets filled with glass. How on earth did it get there? Your guess is as good as mine!

Life, such as it was, went on. Everybody had to do 'Fire Watching' and putting out incendiary bombs. I was not allowed to do this, to my dismay. I so wanted to do my bit but this Mitral valve trouble stopped any strenuous working. So I offered to man the 'Siren' post with my husband. The only vacant slot was a night duty. So, along we went to Canvey Island to the local Fire Station.

It was quite late in the year, about November, so of course we had to have fog, so no air raids until it lifted. We sat in the heavily sand-bagged room waiting for Headquarters to give us the signal to sound the siren. It was the longest night I've ever known, fighting off sleep in an airless room. I'll never forget it. Shame, and there was me dying to do something! As all but one of my husband's staff were called up, I offered to help even it was the book-keeping, as there was an awful lot of paperwork dealing with the Army. Several Regiments were based on the Island. All the officers had to have the bumpers on their cars painted white. Half the headlamps were painted black to diffuse the light. I got quite handy at these jobs. My husband also taught me how to cut glass.

Most of the elderly men left on the Island used to come and sit in the main part of the shop, using it rather like a club. I didn't mind, some were very interesting old boys. They would bring little presents, sometimes a couple of apples or plums from their store. It was still pretty grim living here, a ghost-like town, everywhere empty houses and shops. Funnily enough, with nobody to tend them, the front gardens of the empty houses were ablaze with flowers in their seasons. I loved just to walk round looking at them. There was almost nowhere to go, everywhere was restricted. Even the golf course had Ack-Ack units there and lots of gun emplacements all over the place.

One cinema remained open near us, the Kingsway at Hadleigh. I sometimes spent a couple of hours there in the afternoons. While you were in there you could hear the bombers droning overhead. I couldn't stand that, I'd rather be outside a building than in it under those circumstances. I am afraid we were all getting a bit blazé about it.

By this time my sister had given birth to a baby boy christened Graham. Vera was now going to live in Leigh with my parents, as George was by now in Burma. He had been home twice, he looked simply dreadful. He was like so many having to do a difficult job under awful stress. Those dreadful Japs, the horrible sights George had seen and dealt with had made a terrible mark on him.

Several of the women I knew were having babies. I so envied them. It was rather rough on them really, the husbands home on leave and 'Voilà!' a little bundle of joy. So of course my need for a baby flared up again. Fat chance with a husband like I had. I'm afraid all my jabbing with the needle was to no avail!

1944. As I was still being kept short of cash, I capitulated when several of my friends, who had admired my clothes, asked me to make some for them. I had about six nice women friends who wanted clothes straight away. Doing the sewing helped me to put up with the way things were still in my marriage. I did at one stage feel so unhappy I went to my father and told him how it had been. His answer and advice was, 'You made your bed, my girl, so you must lie in it!' I just couldn't believe my beloved father had said that, I never ever mentioned anything to them again!

Of late, Fred's behaviour was getting so that I now was feeling afraid to him. Not of actual physical violence, but the horrible sexual behaviour he was now indulging in. He was also unnerving in his attitude to women as if he now hated them. He found fault with every thing I did or said.

I at last went to see my doctor as a nasty rash had come out across my chest, and confided the whole sad story including my yearning for a baby. The doctor then called upon my husband to talk about all this, to no avail. He just didn't want to know, telling the doctor it was nothing to do with him. After the doctor had left we had a terrible row and I thought he was going to hit me. I told him that if he would not let me have a child for some reason, let's adopt a little one. Adopt! He nearly hit the ceiling! Never!

He then went off to tell his parents all about the dreadful wife he had, and told them I wanted to adopt a child. They also disagreed. A child they didn't know, to carry their name! When he told me I'm afraid I lost my temper. 'Their name? Who the hell did they think they were!' We argued for a few weeks. Every time he saw his parents it would all flare up again until one afternoon at their house I gave them an ultimatum. I'm afraid I threw a spanner in the works by saying, 'If you won't let me adopt I will leave Fred and work in a children's home.' My God, you could have heard a pin drop. This really threw them. Divorce in the Holmes family, never! 'Well,' I said, 'take your pick, I mean every word.'

For a couple of weeks nothing was said. Meanwhile I had visited the family solicitor, a very nice man with a family. After talking to him, he gave me the name and address of the National Adoption Society in Baker Street, W1. After using every guile I possessed I eventually persuaded Fred to agree to let me contact the Adoption Society and take it from there.

I wrote to Baker Street stating that I had been married for five years without a child, and that I was twenty-nine years old and longed for a baby. I gave all the particulars and asked if it was possible for me to adopt.

After a week I had a reply asking me to go for an interview before a group of governors of the Society. I went to London, found their offices and answered all their questions. This was very traumatic. I told them I had so much love in me to give to a child, that if this could not be so, I was willing to work for them with children. They listened, sympathized and said they would contact me. The time went by, it would soon be Christmas and I had still not heard. Then, just before Christmas, came a letter stating that it was decided that I could have my name put on the waiting list, but would have to have a further interview. I could have danced with joy! One step nearer!

I had been thinking that the bedroom in the loft would not be suitable for a child, so I started to look around for a three-bedroomed house. There was a very nice house in our road, number 37, built two years before the war, and it was empty because when the owner was called up, the wife moved everything back to Scotland where they had come from. Ideal, if I could tempt Fred to buy it. I went to the estate agent and got the price. It was reasonable and I was delighted. As it was only down the road it was not very hard to entice Fred to view it. I went with him, crossing all my fingers that he would like it and buy it! I had already seen it and fallen in love with it; a lovely roomy light house with a nice garden and garage. Fred did like it! I could hardly contain myself. Within six weeks we found a buyer for our own bungalow. As Fred was paying cash there was no cause for delay. We got decorators in, some elderly men Fred knew, who were only too happy to earn some extra money in these lean war years.

Then, the move in. I had already chosen the baby's room for when it came; a lovely sunny back room overlooking the garden. Not knowing whether it would be a little boy or girl coming, I had the room done in primrose yellow and white. Time passed and I still hadn't heard from the Adoption Society, but I went ahead and bought a very nice perambulator. I would have liked a brand-new one but Fred said no.

The following Monday, while I was in the middle of the weekly wash, the door bell rang. It was the Medical Officer for Southend who had come to inspect the house on behalf of the Adoption Society. So he came in and looked at the house from top to bottom, even the 'loo'. Then he came and sat down ready to ask a lot of questions. I answered every one, having nothing to hide. Apparently the Society had written to my doctor, the solicitor, and three of my friends who had known me at least four years.

There was not anything I had done they did not know about! After a very serious chat he said he would send back a very favourable answer. When he left I could have jumped for joy but I also felt tearful. It was a dream coming true. I just couldn't believe it!

On Thursday the telephone rang. It was the Adoption Society office saying that they had a little baby girl for me. She had brown eyes and ginger hair.

'Ginger hair,' I stuttered, 'I can't have a baby with ginger hair. No.' I put the phone down, went back to the kitchen, sat down then shot up again. Of course I could have her, my own mother had auburn hair. How wicked of me. I dashed back to the phone. When they came through I said, 'Please forgive me, I don't know why I said that. Of course I want her. I've been waiting so long.' They then said I could go and get her on Friday afternoon at the Baker Street office.

I rang Fred but he said he couldn't get away on Friday. So I rang two very dear friends of mine who were still running their car as he was an Army Major. I knew he was on leave, so Frella said they would be thrilled to take me to London. That was 1945 so we didn't think there would be any raids. I dashed upstairs to pack her bag. A lovely shawl to wrap her in. I then had to procure some milk for her as she was only six weeks old. I had to get the National Milk for babies that you got from the clinics. I saw the local District Nurse who told me how to go about it. I was so thrilled I couldn't sit still. I kept jumping up to check everything was super in her room. The nighties I had made for her, the knitted jackets, all in the airing cupboard for just such a day as this. 'Oh God, thank you.'

We had an uneventful journey from Leigh-on-Sea to London, but it was difficult to find Baker Street. London by now had taken a severe beating so it looked like nothing before. We eventually found the offices and entered, then I was escorted by a young lady to the person in charge, whilst my friends waited in the outer room. I went in and there were two ladies present, one who had interviewed me before. She read out all the details of the baby and I was beside myself with longing to hold the darling.

They then brought her in, my little Elaine, as I had already called her in my mind. Such a wee scrap! I couldn't believe it, even for six weeks she was so small. A tiny little thing with a few ginger spikes of hair. 'Oh God, thank you, thank you.' I was so moved I wanted to cry.

They gave me lists of things to do, how and what to feed her on, and they said I should have to attend the baby clinic in Leigh, for them to keep a check on her for at least six months. Also I would be visited by a nurse to give any advice if needed. They then gave me a carrier bag with all her goods in. So pitiful, I couldn't speak for a moment. A couple of nappies and two little nighties!

My dear friends brought Elaine and me home. It was now time for the baby's feed. Frella helped me to prepare the National dried milk for her which when mixed was a lovely creamy milk. I carefully sterilized the feeding bottle and teat, tested the heat of the milk and then offered it to Elaine. She wasn't very willing to take it. Poor darling, so overwhelmed by me and the strange room and people. Eventually she took some and then fell asleep. I put her in her pram in the hall and kept tiptoeing around so as not to wake her. I felt as if I had had a miracle happen to me. Now I could look in other prams and not want to steal the baby as I had for so very long. My friends were going to stay with me until Fred came home. I rang Canvey and told him we had arrived home with the baby, asking him when he would get home. 'Not for a couple of hours,' was the answer. Not a bit excited; well if he was he didn't sound it. Back I went to peep at my little treasure in her pram. In the dining room my friends said, 'Billie darling, don't get too close to her, remember the mother could change her mind about giving her up. You have only got her for six months before the law says she is yours.' Almost in tears I said, 'No, no, they won't do that, she's mine.'

'Well, let's hope and pray you are right,' they said. After a bit, Fred arrived home and had a sherry with us to welcome the baby to her new home. He just glanced at her in the pram and said, 'Pretty little thing isn't she. Hope she won't keep me awake at night!'

That night, and for several nights, the baby cried most of the time. I was beside myself with worry. I knew I was doing all the right things, but the poor little mite must have sensed she was in different surroundings.

In sheer desperation I phoned the doctor and he said he would call. When he arrived he agreed with me, it was just the strange surroundings and handling and said that she would soon settle down. To my joy there came a night when she never murmured. Poor little darling she must have felt as exhausted as I.

I have never felt so pleased with life as I did now, when I pushed Elaine out in the pram to go shopping. I duly attended the clinic each week and she slowly put on a little weight and gave little smiles. It could have been wind, but I thought she was smiling at me, her very proud and loving mother.

Life went on, quite uneventful except the war was now over. All the ghastly business of killing had stopped. The dreadful task for some people was taking up their lives again having been crippled in every sense. Fred never took much notice of the baby, only when he was disturbed by her crying, then he would grumble. I tried to interest him in her darling little ways to no avail. He just didn't want to know. Never mind, I had enough love for two.

At the end of August we heard from Southend Court telling us to present ourselves and Elaine for the completion of the adoption. I was so worried that the mother, poor thing, had changed her mind. When we arrived in court our solicitor told us that the poor girl had died. The court then signed that we were given permission to adopt. Elaine was ours! Oh, thank God. My heart was sad though for that poor girl. God rest her soul. I would be forever grateful to her for the gift of her baby.

Now we could arrange for Elaine's christening. She was Elaine Christine Holmes now, well and truly. I continued with my dressmaking and seeing my friends, some whom also had babies or young children. Some of the shops began to reopen and shopping was a little easier. We were still rationed with food and clothing, although there was still quite a bit of 'Black Market' going on in some circles. I made some lovely little dresses for Elaine, all hand-smocked in the front and sleeves. She looked a picture, that ginger hair was more golden now, soft little tendrils around her ears and forehead. She was so sweet: large brown eyes that brought a lump to my throat.

My sister's little boy, Graham, was now a toddler. George, her husband, back from the jungle, was in his old job at the Mill Hill hospital at Hampstead in the Path. Lab. working to find a cancer cure.

My husband's business at Canvey was really down, now the Army had gone from the Island. Some days I would pack food and stuff I needed for Elaine and go to the shop to help him. It was quite fun really, everybody made a fuss of the baby.

Two years passed before we had any sign of getting on our feet. As things were tight financially, I gave a lot of thought to my sewing on a larger scale. I had saved a lot of money, practically all I had earned sewing. There was a nice little empty shop on the London Road just opposite the road we lived in. I could visualize what I could make of it. One evening, after Elaine was tucked up in bed, I approached Fred and said that I had a good idea and wanted to talk to him about it, and very grudgingly he agreed. I told him what I had in mind, about running a small dress salon making exclusive gowns. I pointed out that the town was coming alive again and various balls were being held e.g., 'The Mayors' 'The Hospital' 'The Police' and other functions at the Palace Hotel on the Promenade at Southend as they did pre-war. He listened and said, 'Very big talk, what will you do for money?' I told him that I had five hundred pounds saved up from my sewing and I had a machine, cutting table and a host of sketches.

I told him about the shop which had a flat over it which could be rented. After a great deal of talk he decided we should contact the agent and the owner of the shop first. This we did and got the keys. My mother came and looked after Elaine while Fred and I went to the shop. It was a double-fronted shop, not too big, with a door in the middle. The front room would make a lovely salon with two fitting alcoves. I could see it all. At the back was one large room, and a smaller room with toilets. Upstairs the flat consisted of one bedroom, bathroom, a small box room and a large lounge diner at the front. The structure of the building was good but the décor dreadful. It had been empty all the war years.

Fred hummed and hawed then said, 'Let's see the agents.' At the agents we discussed the price of the shop, and Fred made an offer. The agent said he would consult the owners and get back to us. I never thought Fred would offer to buy the premises, but he never rented anything, always bought. He already had a row of shops and houses in Westcliff. After some haggling on the telephone with the agent they agreed on a figure acceptable to both parties. Gosh! I never thought it would come off. It was agony waiting for the contract to be signed. I was so eager to get in there and start on the decorating.

I had a friend who knew someone who was a corsetry manufacturer. I asked her if it was possible to get any pink corset material as a job lot. After a while the answer came. Yes, and she gave me a rough idea of sizes of pieces and price. After a quick calculation I agreed to buy a bundle, or job lot as they called it. At last we could begin work. Fred had men in to do the heavy work. I wanted to do most of the shop myself except ceilings and repair work.

Planning in my mind the girls I would need to help me, I decided to go to the local school to ask if there might be a young girl leaving at Easter who might like to be an apprentice. I would teach her to sew and also pay her a small salary. I put an advertisement in our local paper also, for an experienced dressmaker who could start after Easter.

Before doing any of this, I first had to go to the Food Office to see if I could get a grant of clothes coupons to enable me to buy materials. This I did crossing my fingers for luck! I got a thousand coupons! These were of course to be spent on materials only. I was so thrilled.

I was working flat out on the walls of the salon. It took me hours to pull the Artex up in the shapes I wanted, poppies and bulrushes. I did one wall at a time, coloured stamens on the poppies, the lot. It looked fabulous although I say it myself. The colouring was perfect. On one wall I had chrome rods fixed for the two cubicles. On these I hung the curtains made from the pink corset material, It was so lovely, it had a satin stripe every two inches. Being heavy it hung beautifully. I had ordered a spring-green carpet for the floor and also a beautiful chandelier, only plastic of course, for the centre light. There were two display windows, one either side of the door. These windows had a raised floor carpeted with green. Pink curtains hung at the back.

The outside of the shop was painted white, with a narrow pink outline. I got a sign writer to do 'Agnes Exclusive Gowns' across the front. After a few more days the flat was finished, the shop workroom finished, I was ready for work and the flat ready for letting. Roll on Easter! I had used some coupons and made a dozen dresses for evening and a dozen day dresses. Opening Easter Saturday!

Easter Saturday 1947 – The Grand Opening, well not so grand really, of 'Agnes Exclusive Gowns'. I had invited all my friends, and they could also bring friends, to Agnes's on Easter Saturday for sherry and a view of my small collection, which were for sale if wanted. My mother had Elaine for the day so I would not have to worry.

I opened at 9.30 a.m. and at 10 a.m. they started to drift in. A couple of my friends helped with the sherry and also the showing of the gowns. At the end of the day I had sold all but four of the gowns, and made several appointments for the following week.

It was a very happy Billie who sat down for a meal that evening. I had used my proper name of Agnes for the shop as I thought it more dignified than my nickname. Now, at home with Fred I must get down to the 'nitty gritty' of the rent for the shop. Fred already had two people after the flat, so I thought my chances of a reasonable sum were good. I laid my cards on the table and told him how I had fared that day. He was agreeably surprised at the success, although modest, that I had had. He named a very reasonable rent and without any more ado I clinched it and we shook hands, the die was cast. I had a rent book!

I had two applicants to see from the advertisement I had placed. Also, after the Easter Monday I went to the school to see if my apprentice had decided to come. The Headmistress gave me the name and address of a girl, and I went to her house to see her mother. I told her what her daughter's duties would be, and they were both pleased. The girl, Beatie, was a quiet little thing but loved sewing. I arranged for her to start the following Monday.

The two applicants for dressmakers were Susan and Daphne. Susan had been on a dressmaking course so knew something about it, but Daphne had worked for Govay Skirts. They also were to start the following

Monday. So I had to busy myself getting another cutting table and four chairs. I was going to have my work cut out with the small staff as none of them had an idea of the type of work I was used to at Hartnell's. However, never say die!

As my father had retired on a small pension, he did odd electrical jobs for me and others. I asked my mother if she could help me with Elaine for a salary. Mother so loved Elaine she would have done it for love! But I wanted to be fair, so we came to an agreement. I would take Elaine to the shop with me, Mother would come at 12 noon, and take Elaine back to my house and make lunch for herself and Elaine. At 5 o'clock I would return from the shop and take over. This all worked beautifully, no one was neglected, my dear husband had his meals as usual so no grumbling from that quarter.

I was now getting busy at the shop. I did rather a lot of evening wear to my delight, they were my favourite things. I could design them till the cows came home! The girls in the workroom were settling down, Daphne was excellent, she took to *haute couture* very easily. Susan became very good at general tacking and sewing.

I gave each client two fittings so there were not any nasty shocks when finished. In my two small window displays I showed one gown or suit in each, with the accessories – shoes, bag, scarf, etc. I borrowed shoes from the local shop and put a little ticket at the side as to where you could buy them. This worked very well with the shops around me.

I had one day a month in London to buy materials, sequins and beads for embroidery. After a while I had to employ two more girls. I now put Daphne in charge of the workroom. The apprentice Beatie was a little love. She took a pride in dusting the salon and workroom. She also made the tea and hand-neatened the inside of every garment.

So, time ran on and it was now November, and orders came for extra-special ballgowns. I did about twelve new designs with rather a lot more embroidery, which I had to do mainly myself. I was getting Susan to do some, hoping she could do more.

After Christmas, trade slowed down a bit and gave us a bit of leeway to get Spring wear up to date.

I was really happy during this period. Elaine was almost three, and spent some time in the workroom with me. Unfortunately Fred was not so happy. I was making too much money and getting a bit too independent! He didn't like this at all. He started his old tricks of finding fault with everything I did, criticizing the meals I cooked and said that I neglected Elaine which was not true.

After a few weeks of all this I was feeling rather depressed when one of my clients suggested I go with her and two other friends to Belgium. I said, 'Oh no, I couldn't leave Elaine,' and she said, 'Think about it.' I did and asked my mother if she would have Elaine for two nights. She was delighted to. The next hurdle was Fred, and I told him that I would get material cheaper over there. In the end I wore him down.

So, off to Belgium the four of us went. I had to get a passport, never having had any use for one before. It was a nice trip across the water. We stayed at Blankenberge arriving late afternoon. At dinner that night in the hotel, I was rather suspicious of the meat. It was too close in texture and too lean. 'Gosh,' I said, 'It's horse!' We called for 'Madame' and asked if we could have something else! She was horrified when we asked if she had any ham. 'Yes but of course,' she said, shaking her head, 'but you cannot prefer it?' Oh yes we could, as we went on to show by leaving four empty plates!

Next morning we did the markets. After all the clothes coupons and shortages in England, it was like visiting Paradise, at least it was for me. I bought some lovely lace, some nylon stockings and lots of beads and buttons you couldn't get in England. If only we were allowed to bring more money out! We also visited Bruges that afternoon, then dashed to get the boat back home. Not a very long break but it did me good.

I was very pleased with the things I had bought. I showed them to Fred but he wasn't interested, instead, he found fault with the arrangements I had made for him while I was gone. I just tried not to listen to him, and played with Elaine and the doll I had brought back for her.

So the days flew, soon it would be holiday time. As the girls had been with me a year I gave them all a week's holiday with pay, as I had been treated at Hartnell's. It was lovely, a whole week with Elaine! For of course Fred never took a holiday. So every day, if weather permitted, I would go on the beach with her, and my other friends and their children. Back to work again, time to think of the autumn collection, suits, dinner dresses etc. Business was excellent, but at home Fred was being more objectionable, muttering about the tenants over my shop. As I was so busy designing and cutting I put it from my mind but knew I would have to ask him what was wrong pretty soon.

I found out when a man from the estate agents called on me at the shop, asking when it was suitable for a couple to come and view it. 'What,' I said, 'view it? It's not for sale.' He replied, 'But your husband wants to sell Mrs Holmes.' I told him that it was not convenient at that moment.

When I got home, after dishing up dinner, I tackled my husband about it. He then admitted it was true, and said that he was 'Fed up with having that amount of cash being tied up.' Now I know that was not true. He was a great believer, like his father, that property was the thing. We ended up having quite a quarrel. All sorts of things were said. I just couldn't believe after all my hard work, that it was going to finish. He, Fred, was in no way affected. The house, his meals, everything was done for him. Elaine was either with me or my mother. Actually she was very happy in the workroom. The girls made a fuss of her and showed her how to dress her dolls. The only thing he could object to was me making money and on the way to becoming independent! That was the crux of the matter.

As he was adamant I said, 'Give me to New Year's Day, then I close up, but I will want to finish any orders not done, at home in the spare room.' I went to bed that night, not to sleep though. I couldn't stop thinking how I could tell the girls although I decided to get Christmas over before I broke it to them. I just couldn't believe it. How could he? Knowing Fred I had to believe it. If it was something to hurt me he could indeed do it. Several times during the next couple of weeks one or other of the girls would ask me if I felt all right. I was beginning to look harassed. I began to work out how I could help the girls when they had to go.

Daphne came in one morning showing me her left hand. She was wearing an engagement ring. I was thrilled for her. She then told me they had got a flat, so there was no need to wait any longer, they would get married on Christmas Day! In my heart I said, 'Thank God' because I knew she had said that once she was married she would give up work! I still had Susan and Beatie to worry about.

I still kept in contact with my old employers, the Baron and Baroness de Carda, who still had their business in Bond Street in London. I telephoned them and made an appointment to see them the next week. I was due to go to town on my monthly buying trip, well I wouldn't be buying much this time! I went to town and called to see the Baroness. I asked if she could take an apprentice and an assistant from me, explaining that they were very nice girls taught by me. The Baron and she had a chat about it, and agreed to take them on after Christmas, if their parents would agree.

Back home I called the girls in the salon and explained the situation to them. They were rather shocked, but seemed to be more sorry for me, bless then. We were like a little family in that workroom. Susan who lived with her grandparents, brought her grandfather to see me. He was a charming man who thanked me for teaching Susan so much. They knew she would have to leave me some time to get more experience, and thanked me for introducing her to my old bosses. Little Beatie's parents came and were also pleased because she would learn a lot more and be able to finish her apprenticeship. So, everybody was happy except me.

Christmas came, and goodbyes were said. Daphne would live in Upminster so she would not have been able to stay on whatever had happened. Little presents were given, and rather tearfully we promised to keep in touch. Rather nice, I thought, they all said they would come in and help me pack everything the day after Boxing Day, which luckily was a Sunday.

We had finished all our Christmas orders. I had about four still to do for the end of January, but was going to do these at home. I also had to sell the Salon furniture and light-fittings etc. I felt as I was cutting off a limb at the time, as things went out of the door.

Soon it was New Year's Eve and there was the usual Ball at the Palace Hotel. I had made twelve costumes for this particular Ball. I was going myself even if Fred refused to come as my escort. It was lovely but sad, all my loyal customers came up and said nice things. They were saying, 'Where else can we get our exclusive clothes?' The end of this Ball was an end to a chapter.

Chapter 4

It was now 1949, and Elaine was nearly four and I thought it would be a good idea for her to go to Nursery School. I knew a very nice woman who ran one, just fifteen children. Her name was Mrs Hall, a widow who lived in Vardon drive near my mother.

Elaine loved it there, she joined in everything and was a bit bossy with the others actually! She would come home with drawings she had done, recite her 'tables' and little poems. One day when I picked her up from school she was waving a piece of paper.

'Mummy, Mummy, look I've written my name!' She was so excited, it was lovely to see.

Soon it was March, and a week before her birthday. I was planning a party for her. When I wrote the invitations to her little friends I let her write her name on them, she was so thrilled. We had ten children to tea and games. Fred was off to his mother's. I don't think Elaine noticed he was missing. I did and was very hurt.

Not having the designing to do any more I was getting a bit bored every evening, fed up with reading, knitting, etc. At a coffee morning one of my friends said, 'Billie, you sing don't you?' I said that I did but I hadn't done any for some time, although I still had my music. She said, 'Why don't you go for an audition of the "Little Theatre Club". They've just formed a group and want to put on *No No Nanette* in the Autumn.' I said, 'I could I suppose,' and left it at that.

Before she left she gave me the phone number of Frank Mitchell the producer. I rang him, and after some conversation, he told me to come along the following evening at 7.30 p.m., to a little church hall in Westcliff where the auditions were being held.

Now I had to tell Fred! 'My God,' he exploded, 'if you join this I'll put Elaine in a home, obviously you don't want to be bothered with her.' Phew! I was amazed, I wasn't leaving home for God's sake. It was only one evening a week, if they accepted me!

So the next evening I had put Elaine to bed and we had our evening meal. I prepared to call his bluff and go to the audition. Feeling sick and upset about it all I went and sang 'This is my lovely day.' Oh the irony of it! I could have burst into tears at the end. The only thing that saved me was the fact that I played the piano for myself. To my delight I was accepted. Now to go home and face whatever was awaiting me. I got home about 9.30 p.m. to find Fred still sitting in the chair reading his 'Bible', the *Financial Times*, the only thing I ever saw him read. My first words were, 'Has Elaine been all right? Do you want coffee?' He said, 'No thanks,' and with that he got up and went to bed. Nothing was said about the 'Little Theatre' again. Now our life as a married couple was really a farce. We slept in the same bed, yes, but he would sleep as near the edge as possible so as not to have any contact with me at all. We had no sexual relations at all now. In all the years we had been married he had never bought a wedding anniversary card or present.

In the beginning I used to cook, even through the war with rations, a special dinner with candles and flowers. For five years I did this, he went straight into the dining room, pushed aside all my nice preparations and laid his precious paper all over the table! When I came in from the kitchen and saw what he had done, I cleared everything off except the cloth and table mats. He never said a word. I was so angry, if it had not been for my precious little girl upstairs I could have hit him.

By now I was beginning to hate him. God forgive me, but I did.

After joining the Little Theatre our relationship went from bad to worse. He used to say, 'Don't think I'll leave you any money when I go because I won't.' As he was mean as hell now, I didn't think I would be missing much.

I'd just have to start sewing again! Gritting my teeth I endured things. As the Little Theatre was just starting and *No No Nanette* was our first show, we of course had no money to hire costumes. We all had to make or improvise our own clothes. Of course I went to work and made four super outfits. These were very much admired by Mr Mitchell who said, 'Would you design the costumes for our next show?' I didn't say yes but said, 'Perhaps; it's a long way off.'

Christmas was upon us again. The usual, going to Fred's parents for Christmas Day, and mine coming to us on Boxing Day. If it hadn't been for Elaine I would not have bothered with anything. I had a tree, put the presents under it, except this year one present was too big. I had bought a doll's pram; Elaine had been wanting one for ages. I was so looking forward to seeing her little face when she saw it. I always made a cake and puddings. My father gave me some fairy lights for the tree.

This year something lovely happened, Fred's parents said they wanted a quiet Christmas and didn't want any visitors. I didn't mind, glad in fact, and I said they could come to us. They agreed and I asked mine also to come instead of Boxing Day. They were delighted. The more the merrier, I wouldn't have Fred glaring at me all the time. 'What the hell is this going to cost?' said my dear husband. 'Don't worry I'll pay, I can always do a bit more dressmaking!' I replied. Having both sets of parents with us made it quite pleasant.

New Year, 1950. In March Elaine would be five years old. I wanted her to go to the Convent School at Westcliff, not for any religious reasons but thought it would be more suitable for Elaine as she was now a quiet little thing and would do better in the Convent atmosphere. I asked Fred if he would agree to pay the fees, and after a lot of hurtful things and threats to me he said he'd pay.

I got in touch with the Convent and had to take Elaine along to pass an entrance test. To my delight she did the things set before her with no effort at all! They accepted her and she was to start after the Easter break. Elaine was such a tiny mite the smallest of uniforms looked like her big sisters! However, in a short time I altered them. I was worried the first day I took her, but when I collected her in the afternoon she was full of chatter about everything. Thank goodness she was happy there.

Before one knew it, the summer holidays were upon us. As usual we did not go away, but Elaine and I with friends, spent as much time as possible on the beach or in one of our lovely parks.

That summer I introduced Elaine to horses. I had a friend who ran a stable and had a riding school. I loved riding and hoped Elaine would too. Happily she loved it, my friend had a pony, 'Tommy', just right for a five year old. Of course I had to foot the bill. Fred thought it was a waste of money.

This year, having no shop, I saw a lot of my parents. My sister was now living in Hadleigh, and her husband George was now a Pathologist at the Southend Hospital. Graham, their son, was now about eight years old so was a nice companion for Elaine during the holidays.

In August we had a meeting at the Little Theatre Club deciding what to do next. After some discussion it was *Mr Cinders* got the vote. Years before it had run in London with Sonnie Hale as the male lead. Frank Mitchell or 'Mitch' as we all now called him, asked me if I would design and make the costumes for it. Someone Mitch knew had donated two hundred yards of white satin hoping I could use it for costumes. Well, you could hardly dress a musical in just white satin!

After I had read the script and saw the type of clothes to be worn I began to work it out in my mind how to utilize the white satin. Of course, I would have to dye it! There was one scene in which the ladies all wore crinolines. I designed the basic dress, and underskirts with hoops attached. Some of the girls offered to help once I had cut them all out to the measurements of each girl. Eighteen white gowns!

So, I bought dyes in mauve, deep purple, ruby red, pink, sapphire and pale blue, three of each colour. The dresses, after being dyed, could have lace fichu collars with a rose in the centre.

Now to the dyeing! Three of the girls came to my house to help, and we prepared the dye in an old zinc bath I had kept from years ago. On the gas stove it went! We started with pale colours, and then down to deep colouring. When you dye something you don't wring the article, just lift it out and hang it. We had arranged two lines across my lawn. After feeling like a witch stirring the cauldron, we carefully lifted the first three gowns of pale colour and took them to the line and hung them securely. After doing the pale colours we then embarked on the darker ones. Very carefully these were also hung on the line.

We all sat down exhausted and worried about how they would turn out. I had never dyed anything before. We all had a cup of tea and chatted, after clearing up my kitchen, which looked quite a mess I can tell you! After a while I thought I would check on the dresses. The dresses were all right, but my lawn – well it was stained with great blobs of colour! Gosh, I've got to do something before Fred comes home, he'll kill me! We all stood looking for some time then tried to get it off with papers and cloths, all to no avail. It would just have to grow out. I'm afraid we all got a bout of the giggles, although it wasn't funny for me.

After the girls had gone home I got a pair of grass shears and cut the top of the lawn but unfortunately it had been cut just a few days before.

At 6.30 p.m. my husband arrived home. We went into the dining room which unfortunately looked out onto the garden. He stopped dead in his tracks and said, 'Good God, what's happened out there? Whose damned clothes are on the line? Look at my lawn. If this is your doing you'll be sorry.' More and worse was said. All I could say was, 'I am sorry, but there's one blessing, it will grow out.' I've never seen him so angry, I thought he'd have a fit. The meal was eaten in silence, he then went out to his mother's I suppose.

Of course in due time the lawn looked as good as ever, but my costumes, well I could have wept. To my horror they were all patchy. What shall I do I thought. After sitting down and thinking, I devised a way of softening the effect by sequins. After putting the lace fichus on plus a beautiful rose at the centre, they didn't look too bad. Oh really they were a disaster, who am I kidding! Luckily there was a tennis scene in the show, so I made pleated skirts and tops all in white satin.

We had a couple of coffee mornings with raffles and made enough money to do all the other costumes needed. What an effort! I was worn out before the show started. This year, thank goodness, I was only in the chorus. Came the dress rehearsal at the Palace Theatre, on Sunday morning prior to opening on the Monday evening. While everybody was getting ready Mitch called me and said, 'Come up in the Circle and watch.' Everything went well until it was the ball when all the crinolines would be worn. I closed my eyes waiting for him to swear, yell, anything! I couldn't bear to look, all of a sudden Mitch claps me on the shoulder. 'My God, Billie, they're marvellous, how did you do it?' I couldn't believe my ears, he couldn't like them, they were awful. I opened my eyes to look and could not believe what I saw. They did indeed look marvellous. The stage lighting had somehow softened all those splodges making them look like the richness of the material. The dress rehearsal passed off without too many mistakes but one expects that.

Monday evening came, we did the show to a very good first-night opening. In the audience Mr Jack Maxwell, our patron, was sitting with his business associate Mr Cyril Tussaud, cousin of the Baker Street Madame Tussaud in London. Mr Tussaud was very impressed by the costumes and asked Jack to introduce him to me. This Jack did, the upshot being I would lunch with Mr Tussaud on Tuesday.

He took me to Burnham on Crouch to a very nice hotel where we had a super lunch. Afterwards we sat in the lounge and talked. He wanted me to do costumes for his waxworks, in particular the costumes for the 'Golden Hind', the replica of the boat used by Sir Francis Drake sited at Southend Pier. Apparently the original costumes for the display were too shabby. These were in the forms of tableaux of Queen Elizabeth I, the Earls of Essex and Warwick standing at each side with Sir Francis Drake kneeling before her. All of them in the costume of the period. I said yes, and would do some planning and see what materials I would need. There were also two Beefeaters complete with pikes to be done! I knew that before I could really plan anything I had to consult the history books. I was lucky enough to already have a book on English costume 1066 to 1830.

On looking at the work in the clothes of Elizabeth's time I had jumped in at the deep end! Such a lot of work braiding, ruffs etc. The men's clothes were wonderful, padded knickerbockers, capes, elaborate hats, stuff that to me dreams were made of. I fell absolutely in love with the era.

The show went on and finished with a wonderful party, and Fred actually came to this, bringing Elaine. I went home that night with several bouquets. Part of the exhilaration I felt was for the job I had in front of me. The next week was given to setting up my workroom again in the spare bedroom. After assessing part of what was needed I contacted, 'Tussy', as I was want to call him now, as to money to purchase a very considerable amount of materials. He agreed to come to Leigh to see me.

We had another nice lunch and he gave me a cheque for £200 to start purchasing all I needed. On the day I went to London to D.H.Evans to buy gorgeous velvets, satins and laces, I was in seventh heaven surrounded by these lovely fabrics. I arranged for a fairly large order to be sent to my home.

Needless to say I was not the flavour of the month with my charming husband! I just got on with the job. I don't know why he was so angry, I was working at home, the house was run well, his meals were just as good. What more could I do? I had to have some pocket money. If he wouldn't oblige then I had to earn it by my own efforts.

I would take Elaine to school, come back and do my chores, then start in the workroom. As Elaine had lunch at school I used to just have a coffee and work straight through until 3.30 p.m. when I would leave to pick her up. In the evenings I would catch up with any household jobs so as not to give his lordship a chance to grumble.

About this time I began to be a 'bit off-colour'. I saw our doctor, who sent me to the hospital where they diagnosed a duodenal ulcer. Whatever they called it, it was damned painful. I had to go on a strict diet, milk every two hours and small meals. There wasn't much I could eat without a lot of discomfort.

However, I pressed on, doing the Queen's costume first. I had been down to the Golden Hind and taken the old costumes off the models. They were filthy, torn and bedraggled, but they gave me a rough idea of how they were cut. Gradually the room was being filled with costumes hanging from the picture rail. I began to dream in Elizabethan times. I had to get the Queen's dress done by Christmas, as my date for finishing the whole order was a week before the Easter opening of the Golden Hind again.

After the Queen I did the two Earls, then my favourite, Sir Francis

Drake. I did him in purple velvet with silver metallic lace trimmings. I was very pleased with how they looked. Now the two Beefeaters, they were so big I had to cut them out on the lounge floor. At the last moment Tussy decided he would have a couple of glamour girls in the hold of the ship. Well from the sublime to the ridiculous! Anyhow I obliged with Diana Dors and Jane Russell. They looked pretty good together. The Hind had a good Spring clean in readiness for the new folk. My family as I thought of them. I earned for myself quite a hefty cheque from that assignment.

The outcome of this effort so pleased Tussy that he asked me if I would visit Brighton, Southport and Porthcawl, where he had other waxworks. He would call for me at 8.30 a.m. after I had taken Elaine to the bus stop for school. We would then proceed to our chosen destination for the day. I would assess that which needed replacement or renovating. Mostly they were replacements. He also commissioned glamour girls for each waxworks. This gave me a terrific amount of work. There was no time limit but of course it was expected before the end of the Summer. I worked five and a half hours a day, never at weekends, just like any other job.

At the Convent Elaine was doing well, she now had dancing and tennis lessons. I was footing the bill for these activities. His lordship didn't think they were necessary.

I was well into the new set of costumes but was feeling really under the weather. I could not shake off a depression. I began to have very bad headaches, also I was taking more pills than food it seemed to me. Still I must struggle on, I had quite a few costumes to finish.

All this time, being of an affectionate and loving nature I so dearly longed for an arm around my shoulders. A lovely hug would have worked wonders for me! I had been starved of affection for so many years. I could have gone up to a strange man and said, 'Please, please hug me!' Of course I never did. The agony I was suffering never showed in my face. All my life whatever has happened to me, people have always said, 'You do look well Billie.' Therefore I never received sympathy. Nobody believed I needed any!

A couple of years went by and I did a few costumes for Tussy. My health was no better. Elaine was growing up. Some of my happiest hours were spent in helping her with her homework for school. I loved history and English. We studied together and I gave her mental arithmetic tests, spelling tests, it was a joy to me. I did so love this little daughter.

At night I dreamt quite a bit and it seemed always somewhere in whatever dream I had, a little boy figured. He had brown eyes and dark curly hair. It was very weird, if I was just sitting alone anywhere, even on a beach, I would be very conscious of him beside me. I never told anyone about this as I thought they would think I was going round the bend. Perhaps it was because I always yearned to have a little boy of my own. Somehow or other it seemed to lessen my depression, like a little ray of light somewhere inside of me. I struggled on trying to make the best of things.

1955 dawned, the year Elaine must take the Eleven Plus exam. Together we did two hours' homework each night. By the time she had to do the exam I could have taken it also! To my delight, perhaps Fred's also although he never said, Elaine passed to go to the Grammar School, Westcliff High School for Girls. I was so proud of her! All the excitement of a new school uniform, sports equipment, satchel, etc. She settled in very well and made several new friends, but was not all that keen on hockey!

Life settled down until one morning the phone rang, and it was Tussy. He was in town and asked if I could meet him. I agreed and we met at the Yacht Club where Jack Maxwell was a member, and who was there also. There was an air of excitement about them, so after ordering a drink they started to tell me all about it. In Manchester there was a place called Belle Vue, apparently, and Tussy and Jack had bought a concession there and wanted to open a waxworks. The building they had bought had to be altered a great deal to house a waxworks. They hoped to open the place by Whit Monday 1956, so they had just a year to alter the place, decorate it and find costumes. I could see what was in their minds, but at that moment I felt too ill to even think about it. Anyway, I listened while they listed the people they wanted in the waxworks. I agreed it sounded excellent but asked where I fitted in. 'You make or buy the costumes, Billie, and perhaps design the décor.'

In the discussion I got rather carried away while I visualized the whole thing. They said they would have Liberace, and what did I suggest for him? Of course my imagination ran riot as usual. I could see lovely drapes, a white grand piano, the candlesticks etc. 'OK, you win, I'll do it,' I said, thinking that I wanted my brains tested!

It was decided that when the building was finished they would take me there to decide on the décor. Meanwhile, they gave me a list of the people they wanted to have. There was the Queen and some of the Royal Family, Members of Parliament such as Churchill, Gaitskill, Bessie Braddock, Bevin. There were film stars like Danny Kaye, Bing Crosby, Diana Dors, Marilyn Monroe and Jane Russell. Lord Mountbatten, DeGaul and Montgomery represented the Army and Navy. In the Chamber of Horrors it was planned to have Haigh the murderer, the Witches of Cawdor and the Devil. There were many more, such as Gandhi, Nehru, Princess Grace of Monaco, Lady Docker and Jeremy Hawk from television.

Quite a lot I decided I could buy at Moss Bros. in London. Jewellery I could get at Whites in the City and curtains and drapes in Leigh. I had to work in conjunction with the wax modellers to get measurements and positions of the models. I had to get busy now on the designs needed.

I did the three glamour girls, Dors in pink lace and tulle, Monroe in white satin and embroidery, and Russell in sapphire blue and sequins. I gave Lady Docker a beige lace skirt and jacket trimmed with imitation mink on the three-quarter sleeves, and a large picture hat and gloves with a clutch bag to complete the ensemble.

For Princess Grace of Monaco I did a beautiful white organdie dress with three billowing skirts all embroidered in silver. It was a dream of a dress. When it was finished I had a photo of myself in it which I still have.

For Bessie Braddock I did quite a nice design, a navy silk suit with an abstract design on it. White gloves, a neat little hat and bag. The Royals, now that needed some thinking about. For the Queen I did a dress that was very similar to her Coronation dress. No so elaborate of course but I'm proud to say it was beautiful, as I was told by my 'Bosses' Tussy and

Jack. Of course I did the semi-crinoline that our dear Queen Mother loves, pale blue with flying panels at the back. I bought long white gloves and shoes for all of them.

An interesting point about the wax figures, shoes, was that they have to have a hole made in the bottom to match up with the hole in the figures' feet, to fit into wooden pins in the floor. This is so that they don't fall over! I'd never thought of that before.

One day Jack Maxwell phoned to ask when I could go to Manchester to see the building as it was getting near completion. We arranged to go on a Saturday and my mother would have Elaine. My husband always worked all day on Saturdays at his Builders Merchants business which he still ran on Canvey Island, so I would not be putting him out.

We left Leigh the next Saturday morning at 8 a.m. We went on the M1 motorway which was quite new. It took an hour to get to Manchester on the M1, then on to Belle Vue which was on the outskirts of the town. Nowadays one would call Belle Vue a Leisure Park, roughly eighty acres of land given over to a zoo, a hall for concerts, water chute, restaurants, beautiful gardens, fun-fairs, the lot.

Now it was going to have a 'Waxworks'. It took quite a stretch of the imagination to work out where to put things. We had to have a longish room for the Cabinet Ministers, a Royal stand, a room for Liberace with his grand piano. So many smaller ones for the odd one or two figures. Also there was a basement which I immediately wanted for the Horrors. After talks with the building foreman and his men, we drew up a plan. All very exciting, as this was my first experience of this kind of thing. We had a quick meal then returned to Leigh.

My next trip with Jack was to the wax modellers, somewhere on the outskirts of London, which was most interesting. Some people will be co-operative with the modeller but if not, he has to go by photographs and given measurements. Each one has to give their approval and permission to be shown. I came away with the measurements I needed so was eager to start work.

After a week or two, I engaged a couple of my friends who were interested, to work two afternoons a week to help with hemming and neatening. This allowed me to start something else.

After the bulk of the work was finished it was August and Elaine was home from school. I was tempted to down tools altogether, but decided to have three days a week with Elaine doing our own thing. This year she had made a lot of new friends and was invited out quite a lot, sometimes for the whole day. Elaine used to spend a lot of time with my friends the 'Cherrys' whose son Clive had almost grown up with her. They were like brother and sister. I did so enjoy these days off work as I was still troubled with my ulcer, also I was anaemic. This obviously was the reason I was feeling so tired.

Elaine had now gone back to school. The costumes were almost finished so I thought I ought to go to Moss Bros. about all the sports outfits, uniforms and men's suits I needed. Here they were charming to me. I ordered Pat Smythe's jodhpurs, jacket and accessories. Stirling Moss's overalls and goggles. Uniforms for Lord Mountbatten, Montgomery and De Gaulle. Also suits for Churchill, Bevin, Liberace, Haigh and Jeremy Hawk. An evening suit was also ordered for Prince Philip. I gave all the measurements they would need to complete the order.

The two men who were assigned to handle the order were very interested to hear all about Bell Vue Waxworks. After a bit they asked me if there was anything else I would like, and I rather saucily replied, 'I would like a cup of tea!' 'Certainly,' was the answer. Along came a man with a tray complete with tea and biscuits. After I finished the tea the manager came and escorted me to the door, saying that he would personally supervise my order.

When I arrived home I was so pleased with the way I had been treated I wrote a letter to the Head Office telling them how wonderful the staff were. A few days later I received a book called 'The Whitbread Book of Horses' with their compliments. I had mentioned my love of horses in our conversation but had no idea they had listened so well.

I had another interesting costume to make, the Devil for the Chamber of Horrors. I was sent a sketch of him and also his measurements! I decided to make him a red outfit including a skull-cap. I would also give him a black cape lined with red. I eased up on the work as I was ahead of myself. Just as well, as things on the home front were not all that good. Fred was beginning to be very erratic in his behaviour, coming home at different times each day. Sometimes earlier, but more often later.

One Saturday afternoon, Elaine being out for the day with friends, I thought I'd have a little trip to Canvey, call on a girl friend or two and then come home with Fred. I caught the 2.30 bus to Canvey and arrived about 3 p.m. On arriving at the office I asked for Fred. His brother Ernest looked a bit nonplussed. I said, 'Well is he here?'

'I'll have a look in the yard,' said Ernest. The assistant manager came in the office, and I repeated my question.

'No, Mrs Holmes, he went off at lunchtime, I thought he was going home,' he said.

Ernest came back at that point, and both men looked at each other, a question in their eyes. Ernest said, 'I'll phone your home Billie, perhaps he's there now.' He did and there was no reply. I began to feel there was something going on by the attitude of both men.

'OK,' I said, 'I'll go and visit my friends,' and left it at that. I didn't stay long at my friend's as I felt rather mystified by the two men's actions and eye expressions.

I got home about 5 p.m., no Fred. Not long after one of my friends called to see me. While she was there I got her to ring Canvey and ask for Fred. This she did, and was told that he was out on business! Eventually he got home at 9.30 p.m. I had kept his meal for him, but he said he wasn't hungry. He gave no real excuse when I asked what kept him, just said he went out with one of the men to deliver something. I left the room and nothing more was said about it, but I did a spot of thinking.

Life went on and gradually the costumes were finished. I had found a tarnished silver chandelier for the mock grand piano I had got someone to make for me. I had this painted white and stored it in Jack's garage in Thorpe Bay. The window drapes for behind the piano, I had made by the Irish Linen House. Liberace's jacket lapels I covered with silver sequins, and also down the side of his trouser legs. I bought a man's white shirt, cut off the tail, and made it into a frill for the front. The rest of the furniture needed for the displays was obtained by Tussy or Jack in

Manchester and stored there.

Christmas again, but the week before, Fred was missing quite a lot. Every time I phoned Canvey, or got a friend to phone and ask for him, he was never there. However, we had our usual Christmas, with now both sets of parents coming, which was nice for Elaine.

We were invited on Boxing Day to one of my friend's, youngsters in the afternoon and adults in the evening. Fred took Elaine in the afternoon, but didn't return until after the time we should have been at my friend's house. I had to phone and explain, and they said one of them would come and fetch me. Fred turned up two hours late at my friend's, had some cock and bull story as to why he was late. It was obvious he had been drinking and didn't know how to excuse himself. However my friends were very kind and understanding and left it at that.

When we got home that night to my consternation he wanted to make love to me. He was very aggressive, demanding unusual things of me. I hated it; there was nothing gentle or loving about his behaviour. I just couldn't understand him, he wasn't the same man. From being totally undemonstrative he was like an animal, no love but hate in his actions. I was very afraid of him. The next day I felt so ill, tired and distraught. I told Elaine that I thought I had caught a cold, to account for my appearance.

A week after Christmas, Jack Maxwell phoned and asked if I could attend a meeting at the office on Pier Hill. I said I would, and duly presented myself. There was Tussy, Jack, Stuart (Jack's brother) and another man who I had not met. I was introduced to Stuart and the other man who was a shareholder. We discussed the state of things. The building had now been completed, furniture in place and décor finished. We were just waiting for the wax models which would be delivered direct to Belle Vue when ready in about 10 days.

There was one big snag. Tussy had advertised for a manager but up until now none of those he had interviewed had been acceptable. The main point being it had to be someone very trustworthy. They were really desperate now, saying that one of them would have to do the job for the time being. As in a dream I heard a voice say, 'How about me?' It couldn't be me, it just could not. I never meant it! Or did I? Wasn't it just the thing?

The doctor only last week had said, 'If you don't get away soon Mrs Holmes I dread to think what might happen to you.'

This was it! A job, independence, but at what a price! The men were highly delighted. 'Just the job,' said Jack, 'someone we can trust.' I was still in a daze thinking how I could do this.

Jack ran me home, full of wonderful ideas, I just didn't listen. I was trying to sort out my thoughts. How to tell Fred and how to tell Elaine. How about school! God, I just could not think straight. I went to bed that night very troubled to say the least.

Next morning I rang a friend of mine who was on the Education Committee. Please Bob can you help me! I told him everything. He and his wife already knew the life I had been putting up with. He said he would see what he could do about a transfer for Elaine from Westcliff High to a similar school at Manchester.

I rang a couple of my women friends and told them what I had done! Remarks were, 'Oh Billie!' 'Gosh aren't you brave!' 'Do you want any help?' Bless them, I certainly did want help.

I had yet to tell Elaine. I explained the position and said Uncle Bob was going to arrange a transfer.

'How do you feel about it Dear?' I asked.

'Does it mean leaving Dad here?' she said.

I replied, 'Yes, Elaine, that's the point of going.'

'Good, well I'm jolly glad.' After which she hugged me. I'm afraid I was so moved I just couldn't speak.

My friend's husband, Bob, arranged for Elaine to attend Levenshulme High School for Girls. Oh thank God for my dear friends. I paid a visit to Westcliff High School and had a chat with the Headmistress. I told her of the life we were putting up with. She sympathized with me and hoped we would be happier.

I began secretly packing all my books, knick-knacks and clothes that were not needed at the moment. Nothing of course that Fred would miss. All my personal things, and the same for Elaine.

By now all my friends knew, but no one breathed a word to Fred. I had decided not to say anything, just go! We were opening at Belle Vue on

Easter Saturday 1957.

One week before, all Elaine's and my things were safely at my mother's waiting to be sent on to Manchester, when I knew where we would be living. The day before we left I cleaned and tidied the house and stocked the fridge with food. Next day I prepared a meal for Fred to have in the evening.

At 10.30 a.m. all my friends arrived and some took more of my belongings to my mother's. After that we all had sherry and coffee to wish us luck. Most of them were tearful until one of them said, 'Aren't you going to leave Fred a note, Billie?'

'Oh God,' I said, 'I'd forgotten all about that. I haven't got any paper.'

My friend went next door to get some and they were all calling out things to write. Most of us were giggling but near to hysterics. We had all been friends for years and gone through the war together. They all hated Fred for what he had done to me. I just wrote that, 'I just couldn't go on any more. Your meal is prepared. The rest of your miserable housekeeping money is on the top of the fridge. Billie and Elaine.'

They all came to Leigh station in their cars, Elaine and I in Louise's car. All came on the platform and waved until we could see them no more. I sat opposite Elaine, we smiled tremulously at each other and reached across and held hands. Oh God, I thought, what had I done?

Chapter 5

We had to change trains in London. When we got to Manchester Central, Tussy, dear old Tussy, was waiting at the side of the ticket collector.

'Come along we're going to the Midland Hotel where you will spend the night.'

We went outside to his car, loaded our luggage in the boot and off we went. The Hotel was very grand and comfortable. We had a large double room nicely furnished. Tussy left us to unpack and have a little rest. He would return at 6.30 p.m. when we would have dinner in the Hotel with him. This we did and it was most enjoyable.

Next morning at 9.30 a.m. he called for us and took us to our flat. Now Tussy had taken the flat without seeing it. The flat was in Rusholme, a very poor district in Manchester. Dirty, shabby, not at all like Leigh-on-Sea.

'Never mind darlings, I'll get you a nicer one as soon as I can,' he said. He left us to settle ourselves in and get an early night after our traumatic day.

The flat consisted of one bedroom, kitchen and bathroom, plus one room big enough to serve as dining room as well as lounge. I looked around and saw that there were several items I just had to buy. One was a new mattress. We were not sleeping on that dirty thing. There was a shortage of kitchen utensils also.

Tussy took us shopping. I explained to the people in the shop where we bought the mattress the situation and, bless their hearts, they promised to deliver it by evening.

Downstairs was let to a young, recently married couple who hoped to be moving in the near future. They were very friendly and showed us their flat. It was nicer than ours. It had two bedrooms, kitchen and bathroom plus the same lounge-cum-diner that we had. Well, I thought, perhaps I could have a word with the agent and I could take over their flat when they left. The only really good thing about Rusholme was that it was not far from Elaine's new school.

We were taken to see Belle Vue the next day, as Elaine was not due at the school until after Easter, she came along to help. I was very pleased with the décor and at once started hanging Liberace's curtains. It was wonderful dressing the models, fortunately everything fitted perfectly. There was one nasty moment when one of the men in the Chamber of Horrors called me. I went down to see what was wrong. He said, 'The devil's costume is all wrong; I can't get it on him.' My God, my heart sunk! When I looked, the idiot was trying to force it on back to front! He thought the zip should be at the front.

No more scares, things were going beautifully. Elaine was having a lovely time putting the stockings on all the women – no tights then – and finding the shoes that went with the outfits. There were also gloves to be fitted on the hands, very fiddly this.

We all broke for lunch and Tussy took Elaine and me to a restaurant, then back again, there was so much to do.

Two more days then Wham! Saturday Opening Day. We had quite a lot of interest shown by the newspapers. We were nearly ready for some inside pictures the Press were clamouring for.

At last, Saturday! Elaine and I packed our lunches, Elaine took a book for when she got bored. What a hope! She was invaluable, a real help. All the workers got very fond of her. I had spend many anxious hours wondering how I was going to get the people into *my* waxworks, as I now thought of it. I just wasn't the type of woman to stand outside and shout 'Roll up, come and see the show!' In the end I stopped worrying and thought something would occur to me at the time! At 10 o'clock we opened the doors. The workmen had all gone, Tussy, Jack and Stuart were still with us. To my amazement the three of them came to me and said, 'Well Billie it's all yours. Good luck, and then left! I couldn't believe it! Oh what shall I do now?

The cashier was in her cubby hole ready to sell tickets. But who was going to buy them? No one outside seemed to want to come in, but one or two people were looking at our window where we had a scene from the Spanish Inquisition. This was quite gruesome.

Well, I gave it a thought and decided I would take the bull by the horns and go and talk to them, and somehow entice them inside. I was so upset, after I said my little piece they moved away. Why? I only said, 'Do come in, there are some lovely exhibits inside.'

I retreated into the doorway feeling utterly foolish. Then I thought what the heck. Before I could do anything a coach had come into the big entrance opposite the Waxworks and stopped. Only two men got out, and after a bit of talking came over to my window and were looking in. Come on, Bill, I said to myself, this is your big chance. So, putting on a nice smile I went to them and said the first thing that came into my head.

'Hello, we've got some jolly good people inside. Why not take a look?' They turned to look at me and after an agonizing minute or two I heard them say, 'Why not?' One of them turned towards the coach, waved, and to my amazement thirty or more men got off and came straight to the Waxworks! Anyway they got their tickets and went in.

Now, I must explain about these tickets. It was one shilling for adults, and ninepence for children. I was going to receive a standing wage of nine pounds a week plus – wait for it – sixpence in the pound on the takings! I had to get twenty adults in before I earned sixpence. Well I'm not an Aries and a Cockney for nothing. So be it. I'd get them in by hook or crook, I thought.

After that I seemed to have no more trouble. I just stood in the foyer and looked pleasant. I smiled at anyone looking in, and do you know they came in by the hundreds.

My staff, of seven Irish women, had to patrol the aisles where the waxworks were housed. A very large ex-policeman as doorman, and a darling cuddly man who, would you believe was a wrestler, but came to us as a 'Bouncer', I think they called them.

You would be surprised what the public got up to. That first day we had jewellery stolen from the figures; Mrs Braddock's handbag, Lady Docker's earrings; they pulled an ear off with one of the earrings!

I was getting rather worked up when who should appear again but the 'Three Just Men', namely Tussy, Jack and Stuart. They had hidden themselves and watched as I went about getting folk in. They were very pleased and said how well I had coped. Away they went saying they would pick Elaine and me up for a meal later. When they returned, however, I said that they would have to excuse Elaine and me, and have a meal sent in to us. I was so busy and excited, I didn't want to miss a minute of it. This they did and we had a very nice meal indeed. It wasn't until I sat down that I realized just how hungry I was.

So the day passed, I was astonished at the amount of money we had taken. I had to check all the monies with the tickets sold and make sure they tallied, which they did. I said goodnight to the staff and thanked them warmly for their hard work and cheerfulness.

My office was on the first floor. Here were the switches for every light in the Waxworks. This meant having to use a powerful torch after I turned the lights off, as the whole place was pitch black. Before doing this however there was another chore to be done. This was called 'Smelling Out'. This was because our dear public had a nasty habit of throwing cigarette butts just anywhere. So, I set off to investigate every inch of the Waxworks. Looking behind curtains, lifting up robes, looking in just about every nook and cranny. After doing this I had to turn the electricity off from the office and proceed out with my torch. We would lock and fasten all the entrances and go out from the door in the Chamber of Horrors. I was all right until I got there, then my nerve was beginning to fail me. The torch seemed to pick up every eye that was there! As I walked through I swear these eyes followed me. They did! I could feel them burning into the back of me. God, I've never been so scared before. I almost ran the last few steps.

Back home in the flat Elaine and I discussed the day laughing about some of the happenings. The main trouble I found was understanding the people, and of course, they, me! Everyone called you 'Love' it was so nice, so warming. Even when a conductor helped you on the bus you were 'Love'. The next day Tussy came to see me, to tell me I had taken more money than any of his other Waxworks. He complimented me on the way I took to it all. Tussy, Jack and Stuart were now going, Tussy to London, Jack and Stuart to Southend, where they had several places of amusement on the seafront.

Gradually things became easier. School was about to start. Elaine and I went to see the Headmistress. I was very honest about our circumstances, she was most sympathetic and said she would see to Elaine's happiness at the school. We left to buy her new school uniform because Elaine was actually starting the next day.

We got the information about buses, and fortunately there was a girl living quite near us, with whom Elaine could travel in the mornings. After school each evening Elaine would get a bus to Belle Vue. I had arranged for a restaurant to send dinner over each evening. Elaine would then do her homework. At nine o'clock she and I would leave, knowing that for the next hour the cashier and the commissionaire could cope and lock up.

On Saturdays Elaine and I would be at Belle Vue all day till late in the evening. By now, I had got to know several of the people that had also got concessions. Actually, I had sent invitations to all to come for a drink. Quite a few came, it broke the ice. I had many offers of help. Lovely people.

Whit week was now upon us. I had never heard of it before, but it's quite a big thing in Manchester: processions from the town, the Religious Orders all took part.

We were so busy I couldn't think straight. I didn't have to entice people in any more. Towards evening I would have given anything to send them home! My poor feet; I could never sit down as someone was always needing me. Always having to pour oil on troubled water. I was thankful when Whit week was over: time absolutely flew.

It was June and we had been here four months. One morning I arrived at the Waxworks to receive with surprise, a letter addressed to me, care of Tussaud's, Belle Vue. I recognized Fred's handwriting. With some trepidation I read, 'Dear Billie, I know things were not too good between us but I never expected you to do anything so drastic.' He went on to say that I had better be careful, he knew all about the men I was seeing, as he was having me watched 24 hours a day. 'So beware, think what you are doing. Yours Fred.' Well I never heard anything so stupid. I hadn't got time, or inclination, for other men after being married to him thank you! As for having me watched, that would cost quite a bit of money, and I knew Fred would never spend his money so easily with nothing to show for it. I tore the letter up after having shown it to Elaine who said, 'He's horrible Mummy, take no notice.' 'I shan't,' said I. We both put it out of our minds.

These days we were both very happy. We had lovely times together, no one making us miserable. I heard from Tussy that the 'Three Just Men', i.e. Tussy, Jack and Stuart, were coming the next weekend, and wanted to give a party for me, as I had broken all records with my takings at Belle Vue. By now I knew quite a number of people at Belle Vue. Show men and women, very down to earth, but so kind to Elaine and me.

As luck would have it, Elaine had an invitation to go for a weekend to one of her friend's. I had met the parents at a school get-together and had liked them, so I said she could go. Saturday came round and I saw Elaine off with the parents of her friend.

We had another busy day. One little bit of fun I had, I positioned myself just to the side of 'The Royals' and stood still, not blinking and controlling my breath. It wasn't long before someone touched me. I moved and they nearly fell backwards!

I moved around the exhibits talking to people and had some very interesting chats about history. One subject was often brought up, about the poor man lying on his back in the window, with the two monks holding implements of torture, whilst the poor man was striving to move away from them. Actually he was a 'debtor' and that was his punishment.

It was now Saturday night, about 11 p.m. and I was closing the Waxworks to the public so we could have our little party. The 'Three Just Men' arrived carrying crates of champagne, and one of the waiters from the restaurant bought food and crockery, which they set up on a trestle table. I had brought a super dress I had never worn before. It was a cream sheath with criss-cross pearl and diamante embroidery all over it. It was a lovely dress although I say it myself.

Everybody had a glass of 'Champers' and Jack and Stuart lifted me shoulder high and everybody toasted me. 'To Billie our Madame Tussaud.' I had never had such an exciting thing happen to me before. To be appreciated after Fred's horrible way of putting me down I was very near to tears I can tell you.

Well the party went on, and finished with us all going round the Waxworks holding a glass of 'Champers' and singing Heaven knows what! After locking up I really didn't know if I was on my head or my heels. What I did know was that I was happy. My 'Three Just Men' took me home and when I got there I couldn't find my key. I'd left it at the Waxworks! I didn't care, I was saying, 'Just put me down somewhere, I want to go to sleep.'

Stuart had a bright idea, he thought he would try a window. The first one he tried was a front one, a sash window and, a bit of luck, it wasn't latched, so gingerly, and with the exaggeration of a drunken man, opened the window and disappeared, eventually appearing at the front door. Oh wonderful, I could get in and go to bed.

I awoke feeling rather groggy, and chuckled to myself when I thought of the previous night's party. I hoped Stuart hadn't done any damage. I got washed and dressed to go and meet Elaine, and was coming down the stairs when the downstairs husband appeared in the hall.

'Mrs Holmes, I think we must have had a burglar last night. Nothing is missing or damaged except for dirty marks all over a tablecloth.' Apparently they always set their table for breakfast overnight. 'Come and see what they did.' When I saw Stuart's foot marks I nearly laughed aloud, but managed to look suitably impressed. Oh dear, I thought, I'd better confess. I did and he was quite annoyed. He said, 'You should have woken me up.' I meekly said, 'I'm so sorry, I assure you it will not happen again.' The next day I bought a new tablecloth with a little note of apology.

About six weeks after this they left to go to Australia for a new life. I approached the agent about me taking over the downstairs flat. He argued quite a bit but in the end agreed and we changed over. It was a much nicer flat, brighter rooms with large windows. I took care to have locks put on all the sash windows.

I bought a few pieces of furniture, a wardrobe and single bed for Elaine, and for myself, a dressing table, a bed and an armchair. The carpets would have to wait until I saved some more money. The flat, to my surprise, was dirty. They had seemed such a nice couple.

I went out to the shops and found an ironmongers, run by two brothers. They sold disinfectant. I told them what it was for, and one of them carried the cans home for me. Most kind, but then everyone I met in Manchester was kind and helpful.

I scrubbed every spare moment I had. The flat began to smell like a public lavatory, still it was worth it! We were now squeaky clean! We were very happy here. Elaine was pleased with her room, I was not so happy. I had been waking up in the night with a feeling of apprehension; of what I had no idea. This persisted night after night getting worse, you could almost feel something in the room – but what?

All I knew was that for the first time in my life I was terrified of something I could not see. I had to force myself to go to bed each night. I knew in my heart, that this awful feeling was emerging from something evil. I brought home from the Waxworks a large hammer I kept in my office. I thought it would be useful to defend myself if necessary.

Two nights after this, I awoke with the same awful feeling and coldness. The air struck my face with its iciness. I lay in bed petrified, it was engulfing me, I daren't scream, I would wake Elaine and frighten her. Oh my God, my throat tightened, I could hardly breathe, the feeling was almost tangible. I knew whatever it was, was coming nearer. I forced my hand down the side of the bed to clutch the hammer. I would swing it from side to side to hoping I hit whatever was there. I hit nothing! I got out of bed quickly, checked door and windows. All shut tight! I went back to bed. After a little time it started up again. I went for the hammer and out of the darkness a little voice said, 'Do you want me Mummy?' 'Oh darling I do, I do,' almost sobbing.

I could have killed her. If her voice had been softer I wouldn't have heard her. I just burst into tears.

'Don't cry Mummy, I'll stay with you,' said my darling Elaine, and we cuddled each other. Funny, when she was in the room nothing happened, thank God. After a while we both fell asleep. Next morning at Belle Vue I rang Head Office in Southend. I got Jack on the phone and said, 'Someone must come at once. I'm in trouble. Not the Waxworks but me. Please, please come!'

Later that evening Tussy and Dick Warner, the fourth Director, came. He had been in the desert, the jungle and up the River Amazon, so was a much-travelled man, who had seen many things.

After we had closed the Waxworks we went to the flat. We took a meal in with us because we had to wait until it was dark. Elaine was not told the reason they were there. At 11.30 a.m. Dick went into my bedroom and sat in the dark for an hour. He was very straightfaced. 'Tussy,' she must not stay here any longer. We must find somewhere else!'

After the two men had gone I went with Elaine in her bed. Later Tussy told me that Dick said, 'Something horrible happened in that room. It was starting to get to me!' We had to move.

Next morning I went with Tussy to some Estate Agents in surrounding districts to try for a flat. At the fifth office, we found a flat in Chorlton cum Hardy. A doctor and his wife had rented it for two years and were moving out the next day. Luck was with us today! As the doctor was moving out in the morning, I could, as I had not much to bring, move in in the afternoon.

Chorlton cum Hardy was a very nice district, still quite near Elaine's school, but from another direction. One of my friends from Belle Vue very kindly moved my bits and pieces in a van they had. This flat was spotless, décor very nice, but not furnished, although I gave them some money for curtains and carpets.

Here we had part of the garden at the bottom of which was the garden of a Vicarage. Reverend and Mrs Latto, with their two children, lived here. The flat had two very good-sized rooms, a fair-sized kitchen, bath and toilet. The nicest of the two rooms we made our lounge. The other we had as a double bedroom. In this we put our single beds, my dressing table and the wardrobe. I bought another wardrobe and a cane armchair, from a good second-hand shop. This room had some pretty curtains already up, and a decent carpet. The lounge also had a nice carpet which was deep blue. As the walls were done in Magnolia I decided to leave all this and adjust my other furnishings to blend.

The two-feet,six-inch bed we already had from Elaine's other bedroom, I used as a divan covered with Sandersons' lovely deep red and white hydrangeas material. I also had a tea chest full of books. We couldn't afford to buy a bookcase so we thought we'd have a look round for something else we could use.

This house also had a cellar: I think most houses did in Manchester, the old ones had them anyway. We had not explored the cellar so Elaine and I went down there. You could only get in by the door in the garden. You went about five steps down to the door. We took a torch not knowing what to expect but, hurrah, there was an electric light.

We didn't find any treasure except about five old planks of wood. I knew up to a point what was needed for bookshelves and thought these might do at a pinch. These boards were filthy, goodness knows how long they had lain there. I looked very carefully for woodworm but there didn't seem to be any! We took them upstairs after cleaning the worst dirt off them. When I measured the alcove they were to go in, they were just a bit too long. I then purchased nails, borrowed the jolly old hammer from Belle Vue again, also a saw, and one evening Elaine and I made our bookshelves! Two uprights and three shelves. We were very proud of them. Next we gave them about four coats of paint before they looked anywhere near decent. I know now we should have rubbed them down with sandpaper. Well after all I was a designer and maker of clothes not a carpenter! To Elaine and me they looked beautiful.

Fortunately the crowds were still coming in their droves to the Waxworks so my jolly old 'sixpences' were adding up.

Elaine had made friends with the children from the Vicarage over the garden fence. Their mother, Mrs J Latto, gave Elaine a note for me inviting us both to tea on Sunday. I had to write back and say I could not manage Sunday as I had to work all day. I did have Thursdays off, if that was any good.

Instead of writing she watched my kitchen window, if the light was on she knew I would be there, so she called on me. She was a charming little woman. We had a cup of tea and talked and talked! I told her of my circumstances and she listened with great sympathy.

'Oh you poor dear,' she cried and put her arms around me. As for me, after keeping my tears back for so long this sympathy opened the floodgates for me and I burst into tears. Joyce, as she said I was to call her, said, 'Now about Elaine, instead of going to the waxworks from school she must come to me, do her homework, have tea and you can pick her up when you arrive home. There, that will be one worry off your shoulders.'

Joyce told me that she and her husband had been missionaries in China for years. Their two children were born there.

The following Thursday we both went to her house for a meal. Joyce had a housekeeper who waited on us. We had our meal in a morning room off the kitchen. Afterwards we sat in the lounge leaving the children doing their homework. Gosh! this lounge was really beautiful: a lovely Chinese carpet, Chinese ornaments and pictures. It was balm to the spirit just to sit there. Elaine got on very well with the children, she was like a big sister to them.

For some time now my mother had been saying in her letters to me, that my father wasn't very well. He complained of pains across his shoulder blades and sometimes in his chest. All the doctor had done was to give him some stuff to rub in! This worried me, I adored my dear father. This of course added to my other worries.

I was still getting horrid letters from my husband, these I tried to put out of my mind.

Back in Belle Vue at the zoo, one of the keepers happened to say the elephant 'Rosie' was 21 years old, he believed. I seized on this and said 'Why not have a party with a birthday cake made of white cardboard with decorations on it and candles. Oh go on, do say yes.'

'It's not up to me,' he said. 'Ask the boss.' I knew him slightly so I asked him, explaining my ideas. To my delight he said, 'Marvellous, it will bring all the kids in!' I said, 'OK, leave it to me.' As if I hadn't enough to do.

One evening I left the Waxworks to go to Manchester on some business, and thought I would call on the Evening News offices in Piccadilly. I managed to see the Editor and told him my idea. He liked it, and said on the day he would assign a journalist and photographer; I was to let him know the time and date a few days before.

While I was in the Press room, I noticed a tall, well-built man in there talking to someone. He had a nice face and slightly greying hair. Our eyes met once or twice. He left before I did. I got the bus back to Belle Vue and on the way I noticed a grey Jaguar car slightly behind the bus. It kept with us and I realized the man driving was the one I had seen in the printers. I didn't give it any more thought till the bus stopped outside Belle Vue.

I got off and the grey car came into Belle Vue, veered to the right, obviously to the parking area. I went into the Waxworks up to my office. After a few minutes my phone rang. The cashier said, 'Mrs Holmes, there's a gentleman here who would like to see you.' I said, 'All right, Gladys, I'll come down.'

When I arrived in the foyer, there he was, the man in the grey Jaguar. I assumed he was to do with the paper. When I asked him if he was he said, 'Oh no, I have a car showroom in Piccadilly.'

'So what can I do for you?' I asked.

He said, 'You could talk to me, tell me about yourself. You obviously don't belong here.' I thought quickly. I liked the look of him, his voice was good, and I am usually right about my first impressions of folk, so I said, 'You had better come up to my office.'

Up the stairs we went, him bringing up the rear. I then heard him say, 'I was right.'

I asked, 'What were you right about?'

'Your legs, I would follow them everywhere!' he said.

I gave a chuckle and said, 'You're wasting your time chatting me up.'

We arrived at the office and he told me his hame was Bill Randall, and that he was married with two grown-up children. He had a very lucrative car business. Also, he said, he had overheard me talking to Burrows, the editor.

He said, 'I liked your voice and wanted to talk to you, so here I am. I was intrigued by your idea for the elephant and would like to help in any way I can. Please don't send me away.' I thought quickly, he seemed genuine, had a nice voice I enjoyed listening to. Oh heck, 'All right I'll see and let you help, but now you must go away, I've got things to do.' Away he went after taking my phone number and my promise to lunch with him soon.

'By the way Bill, I'm Billie,' I said.

I was very busy for the next few days doing the groundwork for Rosie's birthday. Belle Vue office had some posters done, and put them up all around the place. The chef made a wonderful 'mock' birthday cake complete with name and candles! Now all that was needed was good weather. Saturday came and the weather was good, so long as it held. From twelve o'clock onwards the crowds poured in. There were long queues at each of the turnstiles. Then sharp on two o'clock came the elephant Rosie, painted toe-nails, and bows and trailing ribbons on her head. I'm sure she knew what it was all about. She came out slowly shaking her head as if in acknowledgement of the crowd. She then lifted her right front leg and held it there for a few seconds. The children screamed 'Do it again Rosie!' Then the keeper held her still while the chef brought the cake out shielding the candles. Everybody sang 'Happy Birthday to you dear Rosie.'

After that the crowd went in search for more entertainment. The waxworks, I'm happy to say, got a good slice of the crowd. One of the Management came to thank me on behalf of the Directors for 'designing this good piece of publicity.'

On Saturday nights I had to keep open until 10.30 p.m. After closing I had to do my accounts of the takings of the day, checking tickets sold and money taken and tallied. Thank God I had a very good cashier. I seldom had to query anything. Elaine and I always had to catch the last bus.

We were now in the month of August and Elaine's school holidays had started. I had her with me at the Waxworks quite a lot, she also loved the parks and the zoo. By now I knew most of the owners of the other concessions, so when Elaine was around they gave her 'free goes'. This she loved, especially the water chute!

Joyce Latto often invited her for the day. All in all, the arrangements were good. It was after she had been to the zoo one afternoon that she asked me if we could have a budgerigar. One that we could teach to speak.

'Please Mum,' she implored.

'OK darling, I'll see what I can do.'

I went and had a chat with the man in charge. He said, 'Of course, Mrs Holmes, one will be ready to leave the nest next week.'

Bill Randall had rung me, asking me to lunch with him. I made a date when Elaine was going out with Joyce and the children. He suggested after lunch: we could go to Mam Tor on the Pennines. There was an inn that Gracie Fields the singer loved, it sounded wonderful to me. I hadn't been anywhere since I arrived in Manchester.

Luckily, it being a Thursday, my day off, I could have a lovely leisurely time getting ready instead of the usual rush and tear. I was looking forward very much to this. So far I had found Bill to be very understanding, someone I believed I could talk to.

We had a very good lunch at this quaint old stone inn. A bit bleak-looking outside, but inside very cosy indeed. Pictures of 'Our Gracie' everywhere. After lunch we drove quite a way along the Snakes Pass, I believe it was called. When all of a sudden the sky blackened and it started to rain, and oh, the most horrific wind I've ever been in, was blowing. I thought we would be blown over the edge down into the ravine. All of a sudden the car gave an awful juddering and we realized we had either hit some boulder or – oh no, not a puncture! Not up here in this terrible wind. Yes it was a puncture! Poor Bill got out to investigate and was nearly blown away. When he opened the boot to get the spare wheel I thought the car had sprouted wings. The rush of wind in the boot almost lifted the Jaguar.

I prayed then as I had never prayed before. Seeing Bill struggling, I opened the window to ask if I could do anything. My God, it was just as if someone had thrown a bucket of water at me! Bill shouted, 'Stay there'. I didn't need a second telling. After a struggle Bill managed, how, I'll never know, to replace the wheel. He got back in the car absolutely soaked to the skin. Nothing for it, we had to try and get back down, it certainly wasn't safe here.

Very slowly and carefully Bill manoeuvred the car, as we were on a narrow ledge. Eventually we reached the bottom. An AA patrolman stood there with his mouth open.

'Where the hell have you come from?' he shouted.

Bill stopped the car and told him all that had happened.

'We didn't think anyone was up on the Pass,' the AA fellow said. 'Did you see the roofs of houses blown off?'

'Yes, we had that doubtful pleasure,' we answered.

Gradually we made for Manchester. I said, 'Do you think the heavens were telling me I was not wanted there Bill?'

'Well,' he said, chuckling, 'they didn't treat me much better and I'm a native!'

This was not the time for niceties, so Bill dropped me off at my flat and he went straight home for a bath and fresh clothes. What a day! It had been quite nice in Manchester. When Elaine came back from the Latto's I told her all about it. Her eyes nearly popped out.

'Oh Mummy how exciting. I wish I had been there,' she said 'but I'm glad you are safe.'

In our next spare evening Elaine and I got all the books unpacked. I'd never before realized just how nice the bindings on these books were. Lovely red and gold, green and gold, and navy blue and gold. They looked really beautiful on our white shelves. On the top I had a brass kettle and a Dimple Haigh Whisky bottle I had wangled from a restaurant at Belle Vue. The wine waiter there was a darling. I had got an electric fitment designed for bottle necks, also a red shade. It looked perfect, our little lounge looked very nice.

I thought it was about time I invited Joyce and the Reverend for an evening, so the next Thursday they came. I had made a few canapés and bits and pieces. I knew her husband took sherry so I had bought a bottle of Harveys. As Joyce came into the room she said, 'Billie what a charming room. Oh I do love it.'

When I thought of her lovely Chinese room I was astounded and said so.

'But it is charming. You could make a tent look charming, Billie.'

How nice to have a sincere compliment.

We had a delightful evening; they told us about the Chinese people and their customs. Most interesting!

We were into October now, and I had heard from my mother telling me the doctor had made an appointment at the hospital for my father. Good, I thought, now perhaps something could be done for him.

When I next heard from my mother, it was to say Dad had cancer in the lungs. I couldn't believe it, although deep down I had felt it was something serious. The doctors said it was so advanced he could not live very long. Oh no, not my dear dad who every Sunday morning tramped round London with me teaching its history. I demanded leave to go to Leigh for three days. Tussy said, 'Of course, Billie, you must go.' I was very grateful. Elaine and I went to Leigh, Joyce looked after Peter the budgie.

Just before he died my father opened his eyes, smiled and said, 'Hello Kipper,' his nickname for me. The nurses said he had kept asking for 'Kipper', now they knew who he meant.

I phoned Tussy, told him what had happened and asked him if I could have the whole week off so as to attend the funeral. Tussy said, 'Of course, I'll go to Belle Vue myself until you come back.' Although the occasion was sad it was lovely to see all the family. My poor mother went back to Harlow with my brother.

Back to Belle Vue, everything was OK thanks to my staff and Tussy. I phoned Bill to tell him why I had been absent. He had rung, but the staff had told him I was in Leigh on business. He was very sorry because I had told him how close my father and I had been.

Nights were drawing in now. We also had a new problem, actually for the whole of Belle Vue. This was due to 'Teddy Boys', a type of teenager dressed in Edwardian-type clothes. Beautiful clothes, but underneath a dreadful mentality. They wore knuckle dusters on their hands and delighted in using them on all and sundry. They started visiting Belle Vue every Saturday evening. We never knew what time to expect them. They raided several of the other concessions and wrought havoc there. I was dreading the day they decided it was my turn!

Unfortunately, a couple of Saturdays later, as dusk was falling, I was in my usual place in the foyer when to my horror I saw coming through the turnstiles, a group of Teddy Boys. Oh no! They were heading our way straight across from the entrance. I quickly turned to my Bouncer and Commissionaire and said, 'Not a word from either of you please. Leave it to me.' Brave words indeed! They didn't like it one bit. But I knew if they said anything there would be trouble. It had to be handled softly. 'Please God show me what to do and say,' was my prayer.

I stepped out to greet them and walked with them to the ticket office. There were twelve of the brutes, and all were smoking. Now, no smoking is allowed in the Waxworks at all. Somehow I had to stop them. Quietly I said, 'Would you put your cigarettes out please. If I have a fire and you're smoking, I wouldn't get any insurance, and as I have sunk all my money in this place, well you see I would be grateful.' Whew! What now? After a silence that seemed to go on for hours the biggest bully said, 'OK.'

They put out their cigarettes at once and threw all their butts on the floor! They lined up for their tickets, then the Bully took my arm in a tight grip and said, 'You can show us around!' His second-in-command took my other arm. I threw Bob and George a look and shook my head. I could see they were ready to step in but that would mean a fight, which I did not want.

They marched me into the corridor, along which the exhibits were. My girls who were stationed at intervals, looked astounded at me at the head of the procession of Teddy Boys. They soon realized the gravity of the situation thankfully, so nothing happened. As we passed each wax figure ribald and nasty remarks were passed, and they also spat on everything. I said I would remember to change those figures if they thought I ought to. I'd have promised them anything on earth to save any trouble. After doing the rounds they left. The bully holding my arm said, 'So long chick, see ya.' Hovering outside were security men who fortunately let them go without saying anything.

What an escape! The chief of security complimented me on my handling of the situation.

The last Saturday in October we were going to close and reopen on Christmas Day. This Saturday I was very busy, Elaine was there with me. She had done a lot of small jobs for me, and was now getting bored. We still had some time to go before we closed up, so I suggested she went next door to see Mr Molyneaux whom she liked. He was a nice old boy, always called me 'Madame Tussaud'.

I had told her to be back by a certain time, but as she had not come, I went myself to bring her back. To my surprise she wasn't there. Mr Molyneaux said she had gone a half hour ago. I didn't know where to look so sent George and Bob to look for her. They looked everywhere. I called the security chief and told him what had happened. He called his men together, and a search party with dogs was put into operation. After quite a while they returned nonplussed. No Elaine. While we were discussing what to do next, in walks her ladyship with a wide grin on her face and said, 'I fooled you all, didn't I?' My feelings were first relief and then anger. How dare she play a trick! I just wanted to burst into tears. I stopped her pocket money for a week. She had told me she had seen them looking so went from place to place.

'It was such fun, Mum,' she said.

'I don't think it was funny. Don't you ever do anything like this again,' I said.

The next few weeks passed quite pleasantly, although with Belle Vue only opening weekends the loss of money to me was quite worrying. Bill was still being a good friend, never intruding, but always there if I needed him. It was very miserable weather here in Manchester, always cold and wet. In Leigh the air was crisp cold but not too damp.

Joyce knew that Belle Vue opened on Christmas Day, and said Elaine could spend the whole day with them and that she would save my Christmas dinner for when I came back.

Just before Christmas Elaine and I met Bill in Manchester, he took us to lunch. Elaine liked Bill. 'He's jolly, not a bit like Dad,' was her opinion of him.

Manchester had some lovely shops. Everywhere we were called 'Love'. I know they called everyone this, but they will never know how warm and good they made me feel. I love the people here.

Christmas is here, and I'm off to the Waxworks after dropping Elaine off at Joyce's house, arranging to see them in the evening. When I got to Belle Vue and opened up the place it felt cold and damp. It was drizzling rain outside. I could not see that anybody would come out if they had any sense! Belle Vue today looked very bleak. It only came to life at night when all the lights were sparkling.

I opened up at 10 a.m. and put on the heater in the ticket office. Black heat they were called, well named because I never saw or felt heat. Several people came to Christmas lunch at the hotel, and visited me afterwards. I suppose about three dozen people. Some had children with them who brought a bit of life to the place. Then came a long wait, me sitting huddled in my coat and boots. Late afternoon a few stragglers visited me. I sat there so cold and miserable. I vowed to myself, whatever happened to me in the future I would never again work on Christmas Day!

I closed at about 6 p.m. and hoped I would be lucky enough to get the special bus, that was put on for workers on Christmas Day. I did my usual smelling-out check and then locked up. Oh, joy! There was a grey car waiting at the gates. Darling Bill. I had told him I'd close about 6 o'clock but never thought he'd be able to make it. He told me he had made some excuse to the family, and had come out especially to drive me home. He delivered me to the door, a quick kiss and he was gone. A friend indeed.

It was very pleasant at the Vicarage, I had my meal as promised and very good it was. I then joined the family and their friends. Elaine and I each had a small present from the tree. Elaine had a lovely time and I was a little sad, thinking we should be home in Leigh having our own family party.

Fred had not sent any present for Elaine. I was surprised because his letters were changing. No more unpleasantness but saying he was lonely and fed-up with living alone. The housekeeper he had, had stolen from him and drunk all his whisky so he'd fired her. All about his troubles, not asking how we were faring. I did not feel sorry for him. He had asked for this and now he was sorry for himself.

On New Year's Eve the Belle Vue management gave a party to all their staff and the people who were concession holders. Elaine and I went together with my staff. I wore my beautiful cream embroidered dress. We had a marvellous time, lovely food and dancing. I had never received so many compliments since my modelling days.

Also at the party were all the Circus people. They were not all English, but very friendly. It was 3 a.m. before it finished, but as our shows didn't close till late it was unavoidable. Mr White, chief of security, drove Elaine and me home. It was very nice after the party, I had lots of flowers and boxes of chocolates given to me, 'Lady of the Waxworks'.

At the end of January I had to check everything in the Waxworks for replacements, alterations and redecorating to be done. Also to replace jewellery, hand bags, earrings and goggles that had been stolen. Oh yes, the public are very naughty! The whole place had to be freshened up for the Easter opening.

Before that Elaine and I went to Castleford to see the Blue John quartz mine. We had to go down in a lift, then we had to go in a long narrowboat. There was only room for you if you sat with your head bowed, otherwise you touched the roof which was running with water, as were the walls. Heavens whatever did we come for? The only way the man who was in charge could move the boat, was by pressure from his hands on the roof of the tunnel! When we got out at the end there were people waiting to go in our boat back. Just one way in or out. We were then shown the quartz in the rock and a piece dug out. I bought a quartz egg-timer for myself and a little vase for Elaine. We did not enjoy it very much!

Elaine had been getting on well at school and had made quite a lot of friends. One of her friend's mother asked if Elaine could go with her family at Easter to Anglesea. I knew Elaine wanted to go so I said, 'Yes of course, thank you.'

A week before Easter Elaine woke up with bad tummy pains. I gave her a hot water bottle, and said, 'See how you feel dear, after a bit.' In the morning she seemed all right again so she went to school. Later that day the headmistress phoned me saying that Elaine was quite poorly and asked if I could attend and take her home. Of course I made arrangements at the Waxworks, and one of the men nearby gave me a lift to the school. That evening I called the doctor in, he thought it was appendicitis and said that she must to go hospital. Oh my God I thought, not Elaine. I could not bear anything to happen to her, she's all I have. She was taken to hospital where they kept her for observation.

While Elaine was in hospital, everybody in Belle Vue who had a car, offered to run me to the hospital each time I went. Bless their kind hearts. After a weeks observation the doctor decided it was a grumbling appendix. The pain had gone and she was feeling herself again. It could flare up again or not. So, she came home and we were back to normal again. Too bad, Elaine had missed her trip to Anglesea but I tried to make it up to her in other ways.

Easter was very busy. The weather was not too bad, some sun, some rain. The rain was good for business as everybody dashed inside to get out of it. My takings were up again, but the strain was really telling on me. I did not know how to drag myself around. I knew I was getting more anaemic as I was so very tired all the time.

The next letter from Fred was begging me to come home and give him another chance. He promised he would be better to Elaine and me. He was at his wits' end, he was so lonely and unhappy, and so on!

The next time I saw the doctor he said, 'Mrs Holmes this cannot go on! The operation will be an emergency soon.' I showed him Fred's letter and asked for his advice.

'What shall I do?' I said, knowing full well what he would say. He read the letter and said, 'I know it's hard for you but you have got to go back. If you stay here and something happens to you, as it so easily could, think what your young daughter would do. No you must go!'

So I went home and wrote to Fred and said, 'I'll come back but I want us to move to another house without memories. It would be at least two weeks before I could come.'

The same day I wrote to Tussy, and told him I was forced through ill health to go back to Leigh. He came at once to Belle Vue. I showed him a letter from the doctor.

'But what about the Waxworks?' he cried.

'I'm sorry, Tussy, if I don't go I'll collapse here,' I said. This seemed to get through to him and he said, 'I'm so sorry, Billie, what a brute I am. Of course you must go back to Leigh. I'll set things in motion.' He at once advertised for a Manager or Manageress, meanwhile he would stay and take on the job himself. I had really thrown a spanner in the works!

First I had to contact my friend who was on the Education Committee about getting Elaine back to Westcliffe High for Girls. I phoned Fred and told him I had some nice furniture I would like to bring back, but couldn't afford a removal van for such a long distance. He said, 'OK I'll send a van from here.' I also contacted Bill at his showroom in Piccadilly, and told him the latest news. He said he would be round that evening.

On arriving he said that he wasn't really surprised at the turn of events, he had seen I was getting more ill and had been worried about me. I explained fully what was wrong with me and he said he hated the thought of me going, but there was nothing he could do. Also, it was Elaine we had to think of. He offered to help with all the packing up.

Joyce and her husband were upset at losing us, but said it was the right thing to do. She said they had prayed for a way out to be shown me, and were sure that this was the way.

On my last day at Belle Vue, all the people I had met and been friends with, came to a little going-away party. Not a happy one I'm afraid. They made little speeches and gave me little gifts. One which I still treasure was a small black leather covered book in which all those lovely people in Belle Vue wrote, wishing me well. Even now, if I'm miserable I read all those nice things they said about me in that little book.

Later that evening Bill came to say goodbye. He brought a lovely little musical box playing a song called 'Starlight'. I've still got it, I've only got to play it and I am back again in Chorlton cum Hardy!

He kissed me goodbye and said, 'I've never admired any one more than I do you Billie. I have also grown to love you as a very dear friend. Goodbye and God bless you.' I stood at the door watching until I could see his car no more. Goodbye my dear friend, if only I could have had a husband like you, kind and understanding.

Chapter 6

Early next morning the lorry arrived from Leigh. It must have been travelling all night. I went to the door to see the driver when, 'Oh my God no!' I exclaimed. I saw it was a sand and cement lorry! 'How can I put my furniture in that!' I exclaimed angrily.

'I'm sorry Mrs Holmes, it was the only one free, the others were all out,' the driver said. It was typical of Fred! Well somehow I'd have to make do.

I called on my neighbours who were friendly, also Joyce, to see if they had old clothes I could have for covering my goods. I went round the shops and found some druggett, coarse material used for covering hall carpets. Somehow, with everybody's help, we managed. The lorry left straight after the driver had a bite of breakfast with Elaine and me.

All our bags were packed. Keys sent off to the agent. Elaine and I left in a taxi complete with baggage, including our budgie Peter in a cage covered with a cloth! We left the little flat in Chorlton cum Hardy where we had been very happy, Elaine and I.

After a tedious journey from Manchester to London we had something to eat at the railway café. Not very classy, which was just as well as I was carrying Peter in his cage. I felt like Marie Lloyd, the old-time comedienne, of 'My old man said follow the van!' fame. From there we went to Leigh-on-sea.

On arrival at number 37 Barnard Road, we found no one in. It didn't really matter, I still had a key. The lorry had not yet arrived, so I phoned Fred at Canvey to see if he had heard from him. He had, and it was nearly home. Luckily it had not rained, so my goods were not damaged. After that I made the English cure for all ills, a good cup of tea!

Next day I rang my old doctor, told him I was home again and asked him to visit me as I was not well. I also told him I had a letter from my doctor in Manchester. He made an appointment for me the next morning. When he came, read the letter, and examined me he said he would arrange for me to see a specialist quickly as it was urgent. Not long after he had gone Fred arrived home. It was a strange feeling, like greeting a stranger. I didn't know whether to kiss him or not. Fred broke the tension by putting his arms around me and saying, 'Oh Billie it's so lovely to see you again, I've been so lonely.' He actually had tears in his eyes. Crocodile tears? It was all the good food he had missed. He then suggested the three of us went out for a meal.

We had a very nice meal, although the conversation was a bit stilted, but we progressed somewhat. We returned home, Elaine went to her room, Fred and I to ours.

Once in our room undressing, I had a fit of giggles which I had to suppress. I felt as if I was having a dirty weekend! I felt almost shy of undressing. Stupid! I had been married to him for almost twenty years! Once in bed I expected his usual habit of keeping to his side, back turned well away from me. Oh no! He reached over and gave me a very chaste kiss and said, 'It's lovely to have you home. I really will be better to you and Elaine.' I said, 'Let's talk in the morning, Fred, I'm too tired now.'

In the morning I got up, had a quick wash, then in my dressing gown went down to prepare breakfast, hoping to find food in the fridge. To my amazement everything I needed was there.

After a bit Elaine came down and said, 'Isn't it funny being here again?' I said, 'Yes, darling, be nice to Daddy, he's trying hard.' Fred came down to breakfast afterwards and said, 'Is there anything you'd like me to do, such as take you anywhere and put things in the garage for you?'

'That would be lovely, thanks,' I said. This indeed was a new Fred.

After a couple of days everything was in place. Elaine was also back at Westcliff High School. I rang my little group of friends and invited them for coffee. It was lovely to see them again. They were very shocked to see how ill I looked. Lou, one of my friends, offered to take me to the specialist. There I was told I needed an hysterectomy and an ovarian cyst removed at once. The specialist would arrange for this as soon as possible at the Southend General Hospital.

Two days later I was in the Eleanor Hobbs Ward being prepared for the 'op'. Afterwards the surgeon said, 'Left two more days it would have been too late!' A week passed, an uncomfortable one, but thank God the worst was over. My friends and relatives began to visit me. I had so many cards and flowers I asked Sister to put a lot of them in the Chapel. Visiting days were Wednesday and Sunday afternoons. Thursday evening just for husbands. Wouldn't you know Fred never came once on Thursdays! I used to read and pretend the husbands were not there. I was in that ward for three weeks. While I was in hospital, Fred was viewing houses and would report back to me with the descriptions, which helped pass the time.

Elaine was considered too young to visit the hospital, so one Sunday she dressed up in her white skirt, my navy blue jacket, a handbag and a touch of lipstick! I couldn't believe it when she walked in the ward with Fred, a smile of triumph on her face! 'Mummy, they let me in!' I could hardly keep a straight face. The little poppet.

Hurrah, I'm going home today! Lou my friend is calling for me in her car and bringing my clothes. How nice to get out of a nightie into a dress. On arriving home most of my friends were there to greet me, thanks to Lou.

Over the next few weeks I had to take things easy. No lifting heavy things or straining in any way. Very frustrating, but necessary for my well-being. Fred had collected particulars on several houses for me to visit. At long last I went to see some. Nothing appealed until we went to Buxton Avenue, Leigh, and saw, and settled on, a chalet at number 22. It was a charming little place, very nice garden, with a stream running across the bottom and a grassy slope which I could visualize planted with bulbs. Luckily we already had someone who wanted to rent our house. Actually it was our grocer who was living over his premises. In the near future he wanted to sell the business complete with living accommodation.

As 22 Buxton was empty, as soon as the contract was signed we were ready to move in.

One stipulation I made to Fred was that he got rid of our double bed and we had twin divans! While I was about it I thought I'd fire another shot, and ask for a monthly pocket-money cheque. Oh dear, that put the cat among the pigeons! That year in Belle Vue had certainly toughened and matured me. He argued but I stuck to my guns. I reminded him that I never asked him to take me back! 'Remember?'

Eventually a truce was declared. We moved in, it was a lovely sunny house with a different aspect to Barnard Road. We then settled in a routine, Elaine was enjoying school with her old friends. Now she was having tennis and horse-riding lessons. The odd boyfriend began to appear at the house.

Life went on quite peacefully but after making some new clothes for myself and Elaine, I had quite a lot of time on my hands. I thought perhaps I could join something or other.

I had noticed that a meeting of the Women's Conservative Party was taking place the following week. I went along, found a seat at the back, thinking if I did not like it I could slip out. On this particular afternoon I was wearing a brown suit, plus a big brown hat. The meeting went on for about three-quarters of an hour, then the Chairman broke the news that at the last minute the speaker had cancelled his visit. The Chairman said she thought that there must be someone who had something interesting to say. How about it?

No one answered, no one was willing to oblige. She looked around the room then I heard her say 'I'm sure the lady in the big brown hat, the one sitting at the back, could tell us something amusing.' I and a few others looked around. I thought there's nobody behind me and, I'm wearing a big brown hat. Help! she can't mean me! All eyes were on me by now.

Full of bewilderment I stood, wondering what the devil I was going to say. All I could think of was the salon at Hartnell's. So, I embarked with some trepidation on an account of a dress show at the Grosvenor Hotel, Park Lane, London. I gave details of the goings-on behind the scenes in the dressing rooms, and the catwalk. To my amazement you could have heard a pin drop, that is, when the laughter subsided. So many comical mishaps occur at a show like that.

I sat down, my legs felt like jelly. I could not believe the applause I was getting. The Chairman thanked me, and said would I see her after the meeting, she then thanked me again.

She said, 'Do you give many talks?'

I said, 'I've never given a talk in my life before, this was simply off the cuff!'

'Well I never, you should certainly do it more often as you can see everybody really enjoyed it,' she replied. Several of the members had waited for me and asked for my name and phone number, and would I give a talk to – one, a Townswomans Guild, another a Business Women's Club, a Rotary also an Inner Wheel Club. I'd never heard of these.

In the next week I was inundated with letters from these people asking for dates for my talk. After all this, I thought why not? So I built up a one-hour talk about my apprenticeship at Hartnell's, to my debut on the catwalk. I called the talk 'From Pins to Catwalk'. I charged five pounds plus expenses, i.e., bus or train fares. I began to get so many bookings.

Gosh! this was a lot better than sitting at home dressmaking! I was doing an average two talks a week.

During the week, Elaine was studying for her exams so had a lot of homework, which meant I hardly saw her except for meals. Fred also began going out in the evenings, so I was getting bored night after night sitting alone. I had a friend who taught dressmaking at evening classes. How she got the job I don't know, she had no training whatsoever. One day I asked her if there were any jobs vacant. She didn't know but gave me the phone number of the person who dealt with this. I phoned, had an interview and was accepted.

They gave me two evenings at Belfairs High School, and two evenings at Eastwood High. At one swoop, four evenings' work! I was amazed. The hours were 7.30 p.m. to 9.30 p.m. This allowed me to clear away after an evening meal, and home in time for the nightcap drink. Perfect. It didn't put his Lordship Fred out at all. In fact sometimes I never saw him, he came home later than me!

Things were going beautifully but Fred was beginning to be horrible again, especially to Elaine's boyfriends. One in particular was David, an awfully nice boy, I knew his parents. His mother told me how he came home one evening, very upset by something Fred had said to him. I took Fred to task about this but he just would not discuss it with me. He was an extremely awkward man to talk to. He very seldom answered you, which used to infuriate me.

This time I said to him 'You are driving her away from us. Don't you realize she is turned sixteen. She is growing up or haven't you noticed? Another point, all the boys she knows are not strangers, we know their parents.' All he said was 'I'm not having them here.'

So, the outcome of all this, was Elaine went out and we saw a lot less of her. Poor darling, my heart ached for her. I had had such a wonderful relationship with my father.

My friend who had the wool shop, had a twenty-fifth anniversary coming up and they wanted to go on a fortnight's cruise. The only snag was, who was going to run the shop? After some deliberation they asked me. My answer was 'But I've never sold anything before.' My friend said, 'If you can teach women to sew, who have all thumbs and no fingers, you could certainly sell over a counter.' Well I thought, why not, so said, 'OK I'll have a go.' I told all my friends what I was going to do. I asked them to buy wool for their winter knitting now, so as to swell my takings! I found I could sweet-talk people into buying knitting patterns. The shop also stocked buttons, ribbon, lace edging, stockings, etc. I showed one dear old lady how to knit then sold her a pattern and wool! I had a wonderful two weeks. When my friends came back they were astounded at the business I had done.

Back to the grind once more. Years ago we had to buy coal in one-hundredweight sacks, which was delivered to you by horse and cart or a lorry. I had another friend, Gwen Scott, who ran the office for her father who had a coal yard and several men delivering coal. Gwen was expecting a baby, and was very worried because they couldn't find someone they liked and trusted to take over. This entailed taking coal orders, giving these to the men, checking and banking the cash at the end of the day.

Now Gwen's father was a funny little man, who unfortunately was very deaf. I always took the trouble to talk to him, mouthing my words carefully so he could lip-read. He was always very pleased to see me, so when he heard Gwen wanted some one to run the office, he said he wanted me to do it! He just wouldn't accept anyone else. I was, after the wool shop experience, quite agreeable to do it. The only snag was the office had to be open all day Saturday. This wouldn't be bad as Fred worked all day and Elaine usually had some event or other on. So I took the job on. I really hadn't the heart to refuse the old man. Actually I thoroughly enjoyed the four weeks in the office.

Another Christmas came and as I had earned quite a bit, I was more lavish with the presents for my friends and relatives. My sister was expecting her second child, and my brother had married and his wife, Angela, was expecting her first. I was happily wrapping the presents in the gay wrapping papers when my dear husband remarked, 'You are a bloody fool spending all that hard-earned money on other people!' I said, 'It's because I love them but you wouldn't know about that would you?' So, you can see why our Christmas wasn't all joy.

I had noticed lately that Elaine was more particular how she looked these days when she went out. I used to pull her leg about it, but she only grinned. I had also noticed sometimes after being at a party the smell of cigarettes. I asked her had she started smoking. 'Oh no Mummy, it's some of the boys that do.'

A very sad thing happened about now. My dear little budgie died. He had several cysts, the vet called them, which I had dispersed for him, he was about ten years old. I do miss him saying 'Hello Bill' and 'Goodnight darling'.

I have already mentioned Fred and his behaviour, but it was steadily getting worse. He was developing very dirty mannerisms at table, or just anywhere. At table sometimes Elaine would leave us. I would have liked to, but to keep the peace had to stick it out. I had tried by working all day and every day, to put it out of my mind, but that was easier said than done. Nothing could help the tension lessen.

I expect, dear reader, you wonder why I keep putting up with it. Well I had tried to go it alone, but as my doctor said, 'If only your body was as tough as your mind it would be fine. Alas, the spirit is willing but the flesh is weak!' Strangely enough I felt dreadfully sorry for him. I know how horrible he had been but I felt something was driving him. Every now and then I saw an expression of desolation in his eyes. That broke my heart, but if I tried to reach out to him he pushed me away! So, I just went on hoping someday for a miracle.

A few days later I had stayed in bed for a few hours, as I had had a bad night. Elaine came into the bedroom and said, 'Mummy I've decided I cannot stay here with Daddy any longer. He makes you ill and me miserable.' She went on to deliver her bombshell. 'I've met a very nice boy, Allan, and we want to get married.' I couldn't believe my ears! I said, 'Hold on Darling you're only seventeen, you cannot do this!' On top of my pain this brought the tears I had wanted to shed for so long. Elaine said, 'We'll get married, I'll still see you. Oh Mummy please don't cry, you know what it's like here.' With an effort I pulled myself together. I saw she was adamant. I said, 'Stay here and I'll go down and tell Dad.'

Down I went, Oh Lord what shall I say, how shall I put it? I put it as calmly as I could, but the words were no sooner out of my mouth, than he exploded. All he could think about was what people would say and think! Nothing about Elaine. 'Well she'll get nothing from me, that's for sure!' he shouted, as he stormed out. It was left at that for the time being. He totally ignored both of us.

I told Elaine I wanted to meet Allan as soon as possible. He was a policeman and twenty-one years old. When I met him, I liked him, he was tall and slim, dark hair and eyes. We had a very serious talk. Naturally I asked about his prospects in his job, and pointed out that Elaine was very young. Her happiness was very important as she was very special to me. He seemed a sensible young fellow and it was apparent how much he cared for her. I just hoped and prayed my estimate of his character was correct.

Elaine and I, with Allan's approval, went ahead with wedding arrangements for two months' time at the Methodist Church of which

Elaine was a member.

I had always dreamed of making the wedding dress of my life for Elaine. She, however, had other ideas. A pale blue suit. So, we bought a very pretty suit, pale blue, with a thin silver line running through it. A pale blue hat made of feathers. Her flowers were pink carnations. She looked so lovely, my little darling with her lovely auburn hair and brown eyes. My friends who were at the wedding with my mother knew how I was feeling. I could barely see for the tears in my eyes.

We had the reception at the Roadhouse in Eastwood, still a very nice restaurant and function rooms. I had asked Fred if he wanted to help, as my money was disappearing fast. I had also helped them with other things. Fred did agree to pay for the reception, however.

Elaine and Allan went for a short honeymoon then moved into a furnished flat until something better turned up. Elaine got herself a job in a jeweller's in Westcliff.

Some months went by and I was missing Elaine so much. It was a blessing I still had my talks. I was now giving talks on my experience at Belle Vue. This was very much appreciated by my audiences. I was still teaching dressmaking at both schools.

I was trying hard to improve my relationship with Fred. I suggested he took Saturdays off from work saying, 'What's the good of being the Boss if you cannot take a day off!' So one Saturday, at my suggestion, we had a day out in the surrounding countryside. There are some very pretty places in Essex and Suffolk. We 'did' Finchingfield, Colchester and its castle, Dedham, Long Melford to name but a few. I was thoroughly enjoying myself. Fred had thawed out a bit. We had several outings round the countryside. Sometimes we would have a pub lunch and sit talking to the old locals. They had some interesting bits to tell of days gone by.

After a lovely autumn we went into winter and Christmas. All the family, except Fred's father who had died, were here with the addition of Allan. It was the usual get-together. After everybody but Allan and Elaine had gone, she said that they would have to look for another place to live, as children were not allowed in the flat they were in. Immediately I said,

'Oh Elaine does this mean what I think? I'm so happy for you.'

Finding a suitable empty flat was not easy. After about three weeks of no luck Fred heard from his tenant, at number 37 Barnard Road, that he was leaving, having now sold his business and was moving from the district. 'What a godsend' I said to Fred. He wasn't too keen to let them have the house. I worked on him continually till he relented. He and Allan discussed rent; by now Allan had got promotion. Elaine was a bit dubious of renting from Dad, but I said, 'You won't see much of him at all.'

Great excitement, I scraped enough money together to buy them a second-hand dining-room suite. Allan cashed an endowment he had and bought bedroom furniture and three-piece lounge suite. With their wedding presents, which they had packed away, filling a lot of the gaps; crockery, cutlery, etc.

On the fourth of June a lovely baby girl, Carolyn, was born to Elaine. I visited her in Rochford Hospital. Elaine looked radiant! The baby a delicious bundle with a mop of dark hair, just like Allan. A year went by and Allan decided he would like to buy his own house. They eventually chose one in Great Wakering, a modern little house with a garden.

I missed Elaine, as being further away I did not visit quite so often. I did quite a lot of babysitting though, I loved this.

Three years passed and Fred and I started going out at weekends again. He was forever looking at cottages we passed in the country villages, saying 'How peaceful life would be living in the country.' I took no notice at first, but once when we were in Maldon he stopped the car, said let's look in at the estate agents to see what the prices are like. We did this and got a pack of 'places to view'. This gave us a great laugh. Some of the descriptions were wonderful. When you saw the actual cottage it bore no resemblance at all. For instance, one said, 'There is a swimming pool in the garden'. There certainly was a pool, some six feet by six feet! We saw so many shabby derelict cottages we decided to give it a rest. Enough is enough!

Some time later Fred suggested having a weekend away. I agreed but said no more estate agents. We had been to Colchester before but never stayed there. We put up at The George, a very nice hotel near the Castle

Very comfy indeed. After having lunch we thought we might book seats at the theatre, so we sauntered along the High Street and there it was, an estate agents. I purposefully turned my head away then heard Fred say, 'Billie look, you must look.' I turned, looked to where he was pointing. A picture in the middle of the window was of a very pretty cottage. It was in Tiptree just outside the village. I said to Fred, 'Don't go in, we'll only be disappointed again.' He said, 'Just this once.' We went in and got price and particulars, and the agent phoned the cottage and arranged with the owner to let us view the next afternoon on our way home. Actually we passed through Tiptree anyway. I said, as I was leaving the estate agents, 'I hope we're not going to be disappointed again, I couldn't bear it.'

'Oh no, not with Cob Cottage, it's delightful.' said the agent.

Next day we arrived at Spring Lane, where the cottage was situated. Here there was a white farm gate, we went through up a gravel drive with flowering shrubs at each side, then on to a red brick path which wound its way through a very large garden, about a third of an acre. At the end of the path in the corner was Cob Cottage. The flower garden in front of the cottage was a picture. The cottage was white with black beams. A lovely old red-tiled roof, tiny latticed windows, an old studded oak door complete with a stag's head above. *If only the inside is as nice I shall love it*, I thought.

Fred rang the wrought iron bell that hung outside, and Mrs Upton, the owner, answered it. 'Do come in,' she said. Inside we met her husband. Both very charming. They told us the reason for selling. They had been living in India for some time, and were paying someone to keep the cottage in good order for them. They no longer wanted the worry of this, so although they hated to lose it, it had to be!

As you came into the cottage from the front door, you were in a foyer about seven feet square, with latticed windows on each side. This led through a lovely white painted door, with brass knocker and fitments, into a huge room with beamed ceiling, and a wonderful Inglenook fireplace that had seats on either side. Also it had two little windows each side. I'd never seen anything so old.

The mantelpiece was a huge plank of oak, about ten inches wide and about ten feet long. Magnificent! In this room there was a very wide black beam going straight across the ceiling to the other side. It was quite a foot wide. I put up my hand to touch it. It was warm to the touch, its warmth seemed to go right through me. It was an extraordinary feeling, a wonderful glow. Call me crazy but I loved that beam! I just had to come here to live!

Mrs Upton told us that the cottage was about three hundred years old, as one can see from the deeds. Upstairs the bedrooms were very pleasant, lots of little windows, nooks and crannies. The staircase was of black oak with a twist in the middle of it. I thought, we are going to have trouble getting the furniture up here!

The whole place was full of enchantment. Downstairs there was a dining room with French windows leading onto a terrace. From this room through, an archway, was a study.

Mrs Upton told me about the village and the people, whilst Fred discussed the structure, drains and woodworm with Mr Upton. All very pleasant, then Fred turned to me and said, 'Well, Billie, do you want it?' I couldn't believe it, he was actually asking if I wanted it.

'More than anything in the world,' was my answer. I couldn't believe I'd said that. I'm usually more cautious when it's business, but this came out involuntarily as if I had no option. We left saying we would contact the estate agent and our solicitor. No disagreement over price.

All the way home I was in a daze! When we arrived and went into the house Fred turned to me and said 'Happy?'

'Oh Fred, thank you so much,' I said and hugged him. For the first time in years he did not repulse me. Surely this cannot be Fred. We then set things in motion and put the chalet up for sale. Fred paid our solicitor a visit to put things in his hands.

For a few weeks nothing much happened then one day I had a letter from the Women's Institute Headquarters at Chelmsford telling me they had received letters from several WIs saying how good my talks were. Would I then be willing to go to Chelmsford for an audition to be accepted for their Speakers' Panel? I accepted with pleasure.

I then went to Chelmsford for my audition. There were several other speakers attending. There was a panel of judges and an audience of about fifty members. When it came to my turn, I gave the audience bits from my Hartnell talk, which had some humour in parts. Your talk could only last twenty minutes. It seemed that just as you were warming up you had to finish. However, from the applause it seemed to have gone down all right! The panel of judges were agreed that I should be added to the Speakers' Panel. I gave the Cobb Cottage address for future reference.

The business of buying Cobb Cottage, and selling 22 Buxton, went without a hitch. The Uptons were eager to be gone back to their beloved India. We wanted to get in because of the decorating we wanted done.

Today! All is settled, we have to pick up the keys from the solicitors and it is ours. We went to Tiptree to find some good decorators, we were lucky and the men could start in three days' time. While the décor was being done, I was making curtains and loose covers for the lounge furniture. I bought some lovely Sandersons material, a deep red background with large white flowers. Lovely! I could see in my mind's eye how it would look against white walls and black beams. We had ordered stair carpet in a lovely cherry red. I was in seventh heaven dressing this cottage.

Fred and I did the round of nearby villages for old copper and brass items. We wanted a warming pan and horse brasses. At home we already had a lovely old chiming clock for the hall. Also, some lovely Bristol Blue glass and Cranberry glass, which would now be shown in its right setting. I was so excited by it all, I could hardly sleep. I know I bored all my friends with descriptions and details of everything!

I began to dig up some of my most precious plants and pot them. Others, which I couldn't move, I chanced taking cuttings.

All this whilst Fred was in an unusual mellow mood. I kept my fingers crossed hoping it would last. He had begun to talk about semi-retirement. After all he was now seventy!

At long last the decorators had finished, and I had hired a woman from the village to come and clean up. When the vans arrived the removal men started to bring in the furniture. Poor things, they had an awful long way to carry things. They had to walk all through the grounds, as the cottage was at the end. When I saw the bedroom furniture being carried I suddenly thought. Gosh they've got to take it to pieces! You should have seen their faces! When it was upstairs they had to put it together again. That staircase! Still we made it up to them before they went. It took Fred, the cleaning woman and me, two whole days to get the cottage straight.

After a couple of weeks I said, 'We simply must have a housewarming!' I would have a buffet. I invited all my friends from Leigh, and my relatives who could come. There were about twenty of us. It was like a mad house. All the laughter, music and tinkle of glasses. It was a grand night. The last guests left at about two o'clock next morning. The cottage sparkled as if we had at last brought it to life!

We now settled down, Fred going to Canvey three days a week, quite a journey now, but he was enjoying it not working so hard. I wandered about the village visiting the shops and the library. I made myself known to my next door neighbours, Gladys and Dick, Tiptree people born here who knew all about the cottage. Gladys gave me a bottle of home-made wine. Very friendly and hospitable people.

Everybody knew we were the 'Cobb' people and all spoke to me, and made me feel at home. Even the village policeman stopped me and made conversation. The village had its Women's Institute so I went along and joined. Apparently they had already received the new speakers' panel from Chelmsford. When I gave them my name the woman said, 'Not Mrs Holmes the speaker?'

'Yes, the same,' said I.

My goodness, the fuss they made of me! Of course they wanted to know when I could talk to them! After that I became well known in the village. I loved village life. So many people had said, 'They won't accept you for ages.' Well it's not what I found.

I spent the happiest seven years of my life here at Tiptree. I was invited by all the farmer's wives for teas. I was even asked to judge cakes and flowers at bazaars. Once even the 'Bonniest Baby Contest' at a fête.

Tiptree had two places of employment, one was Hutchinson the printers, and the other, Wilkins Jam Factory. At jam-making time the whole village smelt of strawberries! We at the cottage had strawberry fields all around us. The Wilkins family *was* Tiptree. They had built a big Hall beside the factory which was used for all the entertainment of the village. It also housed the lending library, the Women's Institute, the Choral concerts, everything.

As everyone knows, 'Jerusalem' is the WI hymn. At one meeting of our WI I was singing away, thoroughly enjoying myself when a Mrs Edie Wilks, who was standing next to me said, 'Mrs Holmes, you have a lovely voice, you must join our Choral Society.'

Since coming to Tiptree I had given up teaching, so had my evenings free. I thought I would go along to the hall and see the conductor about the Choral Society. He was delighted to meet a newcomer, and promptly gave me an audition and welcomed me to the choir. I enjoyed this so much. Once a year they gave a concert. I was looking forward to this.

Our staircase leading from the dining room, had an old door with a Norfolk latch fastening at the bottom. One afternoon I needed something from my bedroom. I got it, and had got to the bottom of the stairs, when I saw a woman going through the archway into the study. I thought perhaps I had left the front door open, as we often did, and she was looking for me. I called out, 'Can I get you something?' There was no answer. Funny, I went across the dining room and looked into the study. No one there! I went into the garden, still no one.

The next day I told my neighbour Gladys about this, as I was quite mystified. Gladys said, 'Oh, you mean Bessie. What was she dressed like?' I said, 'I only saw her a minute, but I believe she wore a long grey coat and bonnet. She was rather tall—'

'Yes. Yes! that's Bessie! cried Gladys. 'She used to live in the cottage years and years ago, before I was born but my mother knew her. Bessie and her sister were both children's nurses. They looked after lots of babies in the cottage, and the study was one of the nurseries.'

So, I've seen two ghosts now! One in Poplar, and now one in Tiptree. I often saw Bessie in the garden after that, also in an armchair in the lounge. She always sat in the same armchair. It was a nice presence, very friendly.

It was now August, and the WI usually had a fête this month. So far this year, no one had offered a garden or venue of any kind. So I asked if a newcomer may offer their garden, namely Cobb Cottage. They were delighted. We had three large lawns, and several corners that could be used for side shows. I asked Fred if he would mind, and he said, 'No, so long as they don't ruin the lawns.' We went ahead with the arrangements.

Everyone knew where Cobb Cottage was. In the front of the grounds stood a White Hart cherry tree. It was enormous! An old gentleman of a hundred years old, said that he had climbed it when he was a boy! In the Spring it was truly a wondrous sight, covered in white blossom. All the villagers used to come down the lane just to see it.

In October the Choral gave its concert. It was given out that the ladies would wear long black dresses with sleeves. Now, I hadn't got a black evening dress, but I had got some black velvet and black taffeta material. I sketched a dress with a bodice and long sleeves in velvet, and a taffeta skirt consisting of two very full frills. To this I added a bow of taffeta on the left of the skirt, where it met the dropped waist of the bodice. It ended up looking very nice, but not too dressy. I had been fortunate in keeping my model girl figure, so mostly anything I wore looked good. I also wore a rather nice diamanté necklace with earrings to match.

I arrived at the hall and kept my coat on till nearly all the others had removed theirs. Oh my God, I wanted to run out of the hall. The rest of the women all had black dresses with puff sleeves, and were made in a soft material that just hung shapeless, even worse as so many were buxom wenches! I didn't know what to do. I felt so wrong, I'd never felt like this even on the catwalk!

Here goes – I took off my coat. I also took the necklace off, but left the earrings on. We all filed onto the stage and took our places. The hall was crowded. Even Fred had come after a lot of persuading! During the interval backstage, several of the ladies came up and admired my dress and one said, 'It's made me realize how old these dresses are. We keep bringing them out year after year! Perhaps you could help us do something different for the next concert?' I said that if I had time I would certainly help. I hoped they didn't think I'd make them!

Christmas was lovely. The cottage lent itself to the decorations. We bought a Christmas tree in from the garden. It couldn't be too tall as the ceilings were very low. I made two large bowls of punch, and I lost count of the number of mince pies and other things I made! All the WI came, more I think to see the inside of the cottage. It looked like a Christmas card inside and out. Elaine was now expecting another baby, due on the ninth of January. Allan phoned me early in the morning of the ninth, and said that she had had a baby boy at home. Unfortunately, that morning there was an electric power cut in the village of Great Wakering, so the baby was delivered by candlelight, Allan assisting!

Off I went as soon as I could, taking some time to get there. It had been snowing quite heavily that morning! I had always longed to have a son, now I had a grandson. I was over the moon! A lovely start to the New Year.

Life went on uneventfully, in the summer the children and Elaine came to stay for a while. There was the usual jam-making, loads of people picking strawberries in the fields. The sweet smell of jam from the factory was overwhelming.

I was inundated with requests for talks in Suffolk, now I was on the Speakers' Panel. I kept them to two a week, as some of the times I had to have overnight accommodation. Some of the villages were tucked away and difficult to get to. I was put up for the night in several old Manor Houses and slept sometimes in four-poster beds. It was a wonderful experience.

One talk I gave at Stoke by Clare, in Suffolk, I was very kindly invited to stay overnight at the Chairman's house. After the meeting we went to her home and she introduced me to her husband who was standing in front of the fire with a little boy beside him.

I have mentioned earlier about the little boy I always had at my side, a fantasy I know, but very real to me. Well, here was that boy just as I had always imagined him. The little boy of my dreams. To my, and his parents', amazement he ran into my arms as if he knew me. It was unbelievable! He demanded I put him to bed, and read a story to him. I didn't sleep very well as I just could not believe what had happened. Quite distressing for the parents and me. When I left after breakfast the next morning he cried and begged me to come back. I learnt from his parents that he had a birthday quite soon so I sent him a book he could keep. I so wanted to see that boy, but of course I never made contact with them again.

Chapter 7

Not far from the cottage, at the end of our lane was a very old tiny village pub. It wasn't much bigger than our lounge. It was run by a woman called Maud. Quite a small woman, full of wit and cheeky repartee. Fred and I started to stroll round there often in the evenings.

One evening we went to The New Times, as it was called, and as I stepped in I met the eyes of a man leaning on the bar. It was electric, as if something had exploded inside of me! I dragged my eyes away thinking, don't look, this is trouble – don't look! I placed myself on a seat facing away from him. My husband went to the bar to fetch our drinks, and Maud introduced him to this man. Evidently he often used this inn. To my horror Fred brought him back to our table! Oh Lord, this I could do without. The two men got on quite well, considering Fred was a 'Townie' and the other was obviously a countryman.

He told us he bred horses in his spare time but was an architect and surveyor. He and his wife lived in an old cottage in a village not far away. He was Geoff, and his wife Joan. I entered very little in the conversation. At our usual time we got up to leave, and Fred said, 'We are at Cobb Cottage, just along the lane. Why not drop in and see us any time. I'm retired now, and would like to chat.' We said our 'Goodnights' and left.

About three days after this, about three o'clock in the afternoon, I was surprised to see a red Mini car turn in at the driveway. Who on earth could that be? I don't know anybody with a red Mini. Then, Oh no, it couldn't be – it certainly was. The fellow from The New Times, Geoff. Oh Lord, and Fred's not here! What do I do? It was no good pretending I wasn't in, because there was a book and a drink on the garden table.

I went to greet him and said, 'What a shame, Fred isn't here.'

'That's all right, it was you I was hoping to see,' he said. We took drinks into the garden. We had hardly sat down when he said, 'Surely you felt the effect we had on each other the other night?'

'No. No, you're wrong,' I said, without much conviction. Oh dear, it was even worse than I thought. The nearness of him, his voice, those brown eyes doing heaven knows what to me. I wanted so much to put my arms around him! Hell, I hadn't even felt like this for dear Bill in Manchester. Panic-stricken, I begged him to go, and told him when Fred would be here. Thank goodness he saw how upset I was, and went, saying he would phone me.

About half an hour later Fred arrived. I felt so guilty and I had done nothing. I was so churned up inside I felt it must show in my face. I told Fred Geoff had called, that I had given him a drink and that was that.

For a while now, although Fred had said he was going to Canvey three days a week, he would often say, 'I've got to go, I've some business to see to.' On one of the other days. I never knew when he was going or not.

On one of these unexpected days, I phoned the office and asked to talk to him. The manager answered and said, 'He's not here, Mrs Holmes, it's not his day to come in.' I replied, 'Thanks,' and put the phone down. Now, where is he? When he came home I said, 'I phoned you today, you weren't there.' 'Oh,' he said, 'that must have been when I was giving Len a hand loading up a lorry.' He never even blinked when he said it. I wanted to say something but held my tongue. Things hadn't been all that bad lately, and I didn't want to rock the boat!

A few days later I was having tea with my friend Olive in the garden. I had my back to the front of the garden, but my friend sitting opposite had full view. She suddenly said, 'Were you expecting another visitor, Billie?'

'No,' I said, and turned around. Not him! Oh yes it was, large as life and twice as charming. Of course I had to introduce him to Olive as a friend of Fred's and mine.

I went into the cottage to get more tea and cakes, and I could hear Olive laughing so I played the game till she left. I said, 'Gosh! I hope she doesn't gossip about this.'

'What can she say, Billie? I said I was an old friend of both of you,' he replied.

'You're dreadful,' I said. He helped me carry the tea things inside, then turned and took me into his arms.

Oh, how many years had I yearned just to feel strong arms around me. At last I pushed him away saying 'Please don't rush me, I'm not used to this.' He said, 'Let's meet somewhere and have a meal. There's so much I want to say to you, Billie, please say you'll come.' I agreed and we arranged time and a meeting place just outside the village.

Fred was home late again. Just as well, it gave me time to get a hold of myself. Tuesday, Wednesday, Thursday were the days Fred went to Canvey. On Sunday evening Fred said he had to go in the next day. I didn't question this.

On Tuesday I met Geoff as planned, and we went to Burnham on Crouch, a very nice place, lots of yachts. We had a very nice lunch at a hotel alongside the water, and talked a lot over coffee. We then went for a walk and watched the boat builders. Geoff had a word with some of the men. We then found a wooden seat in a little inlet along the front, where we sat for some time talking.

He told me his wife Joan was an alcoholic who, in between bouts, worked at Maldon. He said he never knew what he would find when he went home each evening. Sometimes she would be all right for a couple of weeks then Bingo – be dead drunk by the time he got home. He never knew where she got the drink, as what little he kept in the house was under lock and key. He said that's why it was so nice talking to me. 'A fond mother and grandmother, good housekeeper as well. I wonder if Fred knows how lucky he is.'

When we returned to Tiptree, he stopped the car, gave me a hug and said he would phone me. I walked home across the common. Fred arrived home quite late, I had kept a meal for him but it was rather longer than I thought it would be, so it was overdone! When I remarked on the odd hours he expected his meal he said, 'Don't bother to do any dinner for me, I'll have some out.'

'You don't have to do that, just give me a ring and I'll start cooking then,' I retorted.

That weekend, sorting the wash, I noticed that two of his shirts, the collars and cuffs, had smudges on them. It looked like lipstick to me. He was in the garden at the time, so I took the shirts and tackled him with them. He pooh-poohed the idea, said he knew nothing about the marks. Also while I was at it, I asked him, 'Who's Mary?' His face tightened, and he said, 'I don't know any Mary.'

No? I had hit on a raw spot I knew by his manner. It was when I phoned up once, while the man who answered me shouted out to his fellow worker, 'Where's Mr Fred?' I distinctly heard someone in the background say, 'He's at Mary's isn't he?' So there must be a Mary somewhere! I said, 'You do know a Mary. I know you do.' This shook Fred who said, 'She's just a customer I called on.' I said, 'You visit your customers now do you? How nice for them!' I went back into the cottage full of anger and frustration. What was he playing at! I didn't know how to handle this.

The day passed, the pair of us only speaking when necessary. This went on for a week. Years ago this sometimes happened for three weeks at a time. I thought all that was behind us. The atmosphere was so horrible I put all my things in the spare room and slept there. I found I could sleep better away from him.

Geoff happened to phone one morning. I was so happy to hear a friendly voice I burst into tears.

'Hey what's all this?' he said. I told him through my tears and gulps.

'I'll be there as soon as I can,' he said. After about an hour he arrived and said, 'Let's get out of here, away from the cottage.' He was right, I'd felt as if the ceilings were pressing down on me! I poured out all my misery, he held me in his arms and said, 'If only I could take you away from all this.' I knew this was impossible because of poor Joan. Her need was greater than mine. I'll get through this, I have in the past.

Since we had lived in the cottage Fred had been bearable, until a few months ago when he had that 'shut' look on his face again. It seems we were back to square one! I had to give a couple of talks that next week. It was an effort to give my mind to it, and also be charming to the ladies I met. This dreadful atmosphere went on for weeks.

In sheer desperation I went to stay with Elaine and the children. This was lovely, Richard was growing into a lovely little boy. When I arrived, Elaine was shocked to see how under the weather I looked. This couple of days with Elaine and Allan did wonders for me.

On the third day, Allan drove me back to Tiptree. We arrived at about 7.00 p.m. No Fred, dirty crockery in the kitchen, an unmade bed. I set about tidying up and cooking a meal of sorts. I waited up for him, I had phoned and told him I'd be home about 7.00 p.m. He came home at 10.30 p.m.

'Hello, how long have you been back?' he said. I replied, 'Allan brought me home at seven o' clock.'

That was that! Life was no different, gone were the good days we had when we first moved in. He had always been like this, I never knowing from one day to another how he would be. Oh well, I'd just have to get on with it. I'd done it before and survived.

For some years now I had been taking the magazine *Woman's Journal.* One month they were selling tickets at five shillings each for a visit to one of Hartnell's dress shows. Of course I dashed off a letter complete with cheque for a ticket.

After a few days I had an answer, all the tickets had been sold. I couldn't believe it! While I felt angry, I sat down and wrote to Norman Hartnell, explaining what had happened, and the fact that I had worked for him in the past. To my joy, I received a letter from Hartnell with a ticket for the show, also a note written by Hartnell saying he wished to see me when I arrived! Glory be, I was over the moon. The show was in ten days' time. I started to plan what I would wear, and settled for a navy suit with white lace blouse, and a large navy hat and white gloves. Since living in the cottage I had not travelled to London, so after a bit I decided to go with Fred to Benfleet Station, and go from there.

I eventually got to Charing Cross Station and went up Villiers Street, walking the same route as when I worked in London. However, at the top of Bond Street I got a cab so as to arrive in style! Just before I arrived at number 26 I put on fresh white gloves.

At the entrance to Hartnell's there was a liveried doorman who was taking the cards. I noticed a group of *Journal* women who had small white tickets. I proffered my beautiful invitation signed by Hartnell! I told the man Mr Hartnell was expecting me. He took me through into the foyer and told another man to take me to Hartnell. All the fuss, I indeed felt like a Countess.

At last, with my old boss. It was with affection I greeted him. He asked me to sit beside him, he was going to compere the show. Afterwards he asked me to lunch with him saying it would 'only be a few bits and pieces from Fortnums'. 'Oh yes please,' I said, knowing how delicious Fortnums bits and pieces were!

Oh, the show was marvellous. Such cut, design and beautiful stitching. I almost wished I was working for him again. A truly wonderful collection! We all, that is Hartnell, his four house models, and myself, went to the small salon to have lunch. Very good conversation, giggles and affection, ribbing between the four young models. Hartnell asked me about myself and also touched on the days I worked for him. I had left the cottage at 8.30a.m. and had not had a coffee yet. All they seemed to have at lunch was champagne. I don't know how many glasses I had, because as soon as I had drunk some they filled the glass again.

About 3p.m. Hartnell was called away, but before going he said, 'How lovely to see you again. You haven't changed a bit. Do see my secretary before you go, she has something for you. Goodbye, do keep in touch.' After some more chat with the models asking about Hartnell in the days I was modelling, I left with a beautifully wrapped parcel. On opening it I found a large box of 'In Love' talc, and a bottle of 'In Love' perfume, together with a signed photograph of Hartnell himself.

I remember walking out of Hartnell's and going down Bruton Street. The next thing I remember was hearing people shouting. When I recovered, to my horror, I found I was standing in the middle of Bond Street with two cab drivers begging me to 'cross for God's sake!' 'All right, I'm going,' I said, and staggered to the pavement.

I then went up Conduit Street. All I could think of was where could I get a cup of tea, I was so thirsty! I ended up in a queue outside D.H.Evans, a wonderful store. At last I was sitting at a table having ordered tea. I felt marvellously happy and hadn't a care in the world, looking at everything through a champagne haze! The waitress brought the tea. I had my first cup, oh lovely! Then the second cup, couldn't seem to squeeze any more from the teapot. So, as the waitress passed, I touched her arm and said, 'Please could I have another pot of tea, I've hollow legs you know!' One or two people at nearby tables smiled, but I did not care, I was so happy.

At last I left D.H.Evans. Outside I got a taxi to Charing Cross Station. I eventually arrived at Leigh station, to stay at my friend Pam Cherry's house until my husband picked me up later. Arriving at Pam's house the taxi driver walked up the path with me and said, 'You're wonderful, I've so enjoyed driving you. If that's how champagne affects you I'll buy a bottle!'

My friend made me more tea and wanted to hear all about my wonderful day. Sadly, I never saw Hartnell again, although when he was knighted I wrote and congratulated him, and received a lovely letter back from him which I treasure. He died in 1979, aged seventy-seven years. One of the most charming men, and the best boss anyone could work for.

The man who lived in the Manor House at Tiptree had just died. It was he who owned the strawberry fields around us. His wife now decided to sell all this land. Alas, the property developers immediately put houses all around us. From the back of the cottage all the pretty views had gone. Instead of which, we had the backs of the houses. The builders wanted to buy some of our land but Fred was adamant. Also to our dismay the little pub, The New Times, was being demolished now Maud had retired. In its place a darned great modern place was being built there.

Immediately Fred said, 'We're getting out of here, it's spoilt.' After some discussion we thought we'd start looking for another place to live. We decided we would go back to the Southend area, at least it would already be built up. We chose to have a look at places in Thorpe Bay, some miles out of Southend, not too near Great Wakering; we didn't want Elaine and Allan to think we were on their doorstep!

Fred was keen to have a bungalow, no stairs this time. I was also happy about this, as for some time now I had had a lot of chest pains and some shortness of breath. One good thing about this move, Fred was talking to me again. Perhaps it was the thought of moving nearer to this Mary person that was pleasing him.

We put the cottage up for sale and to our amazement the second person who saw it, bought it. Now we had to find a bungalow quickly. At Thorpe Bay after looking at several places we chose one. We put the buying in motion, and luckily the people were moving out as soon as the contract was signed. This enabled us to redecorate before moving in. We moved in November 1974. Happily for me, the garden was a decent size. After we were settled I vowed to myself that this was the very last time I moved house. It was very nice to be here, with Elaine and the children able to drop in and see us.

I began my talks again. Fortunately Fred was being quite amiable, although he still went off Heaven knows where. I had decided that I wasn't going to worry anymore, just let it all flow over me. Hard to do, but I was determined for my health's sake.

It had been hell saying goodbye to Geoff but it just had to be. I often longed for him, the comfort of his arms. Many tears were shed by me.

Now I was nearer to Elaine, I began to make some dresses for her and Carolyn. I also needed a new outfit for my Hartnell talks. I made for this a lovely purple dress and three-quarter coat, with a matching velvet hat. I trimmed the coat and the hat with mink tails. It really looked 'Hartnell'. I liked living here; we were quite near the sea, and could take walks along the promenade.

After a couple of days, the woman next door had called and invited me to her Townswoman's Guild. On the meeting date I went along with her and enjoyed it very much. It was nice being in the audience for a change. However, one of the women recognized my name as a speaker she had heard of, so of course I was asked to give a talk to them at a later date. I had enjoyed the meeting so I joined. The next monthly meeting the speaker let them down so I filled the gap. Judging by the questions and applause they enjoyed it. All this made me feel at home.

Fred was now seventy-five and had fully retired. He didn't look his age as he was slim and wiry. Life went on rather humdrum, Fred still pottering and going off on his jaunts. I was doing talks at some lovely places in Essex. I still did a few in Suffolk.

The phone rang one evening and it was a woman with a very nice voice, asking if I was Mrs Billie Holmes the speaker. I said I was, and she said, 'Well I wonder if you would come to my house to give your Hartnell talk to my dinner guests. I live at Great Leighs. Would you be able to come?' I said that I would love to, but would require transport. She said, 'No trouble at all. I'll send a car for you.' We settled on my fee and a date and I asked where she was in Great Leighs. She said, 'Oh, it's Moulsham Hall,' and we said goodbye. I had heard of Moulsham Hall, what a beautiful place it was.

At the time and date agreed the car arrived; a Daimler with a chauffeur. We drove past Chelmsford into the country. We turned into beautifully kept park land and on to a lovely old country house. My hostess came to greet me dressed in a very nice dinner dress. I was introduced to her guests, about twenty of them. We sat down to a super meal. After, in the lounge I gave my Hartnell talk. They seemed to enjoy it. This time I had gentlemen in the audience, who apparently also enjoyed it.

After a while I left, but as my hostess was taking me upstairs to the bedroom where I had left my coat she said, 'I would like to give you these, Mrs Holmes, in appreciation of your wonderful talk. In her hand was a Prince of Wales feather headdress, worn years ago by the débutantes at the courts. Of course I had seen them before, but to be given one!

'Oh I couldn't take it, haven't you a daughter who would like them?' I said. She replied, 'No my dear, I only have sons. Do please have them, you could show them at your talks.'

Well of course, I accepted them with great pleasure. I'd made many a débutante's dress at Hartnell's but never dreamt I would own the 'Feathers'. About a week later, I received a letter from her thanking me again for the most interesting talk she had heard in years. 'I look forward to hearing you again. Yours sincerely, Mrs Joslin.' How nice of her I still have that letter among others that I treasure.

Time flies, my grandchildren were growing up. I was now sending them to elocution lessons at a Drama School in Westcliff. This school sent their pupils to enter in the Music Festival. Carolyn and Richard performed in this, and I am proud to say they came home with certificates.

Christmas at Thorpe Bay was very nice. The family could stay if they wished. Once or twice Geoff managed a flying visit and we would have lunch somewhere and a chat. It was lovely to see him, but left me unsettled for a time.

It was lucky that we had a phone in the kitchen, as one evening I was doing the dishes when it rang. It was Geoff's wife Joan. She sounded very distraught, and with a shaky voice she told me Geoff had died at the wheel of his car! Fortunately he was in the office car park. It was his heart. I just could not believe it. I didn't see or hear from him often these days but he was always in my thoughts. I wanted to weep but of course could not. I went to the lounge and told Fred, trying to keep my voice steady. Even that night, sharing a room with Fred meant I could not weep. All the grief was settled in a hard knot in my chest. If only I could be on my own for a while. Fred chose these few days to stay close to home!

I had made a new circle of friends here at Thorpe Bay. I also had begun to see some of my very old friends at Leigh. I started having dinner parties again. I adore cooking and these little dos were very pleasant.

My Guild was without a Secretary, and was in danger of closing unless someone would oblige, so I offered. Gosh, I didn't realize what I had let myself in for! I did this for two years and then someone else offered to do it. Thank goodness!

It was soon after this that Fred stopped mowing the lawns. When I asked him why, he said, 'I've had enough! I've been through two World Wars. I'm 84 years old – it's enough!' So, of course I had to do it. Our two lawns were quite big. To cut them and do the edges took one and three-quarters of an hour. Perhaps this isn't much for a fit person but I still had an ulcer and Mitral Valve trouble. After about two months of cutting the lawns, I was having real trouble with chest pains and shortness of breath. The doctor sent me to hospital where they diagnosed Angina.

I was still struggling to cut the lawns at the back. I was in a lot of pain, and said to my husband who had been sitting in a chair watching me, 'Thank goodness that's finished.' He remarked that I had not done the front lawn yet! 'Blow the front, I don't care if it grows ten feet. I'm not cutting it,' I replied. He said nothing, but went straight to the phone and spoke to someone who would come and give an estimate for paving the whole front! It was duly paved. About a month after this, Fred didn't appear for breakfast, so I went to his room to see what had happened.

'Are you all right?' I asked.

'I'm just not getting up any more,' he said.

'Are you ill? I'll get a doctor.' He never answered. He stayed there for a week, not eating or drinking very much. I called in at the doctors and explained matters. He knew how cantankerous a man he was, so he said, 'Just ignore him, he'll get bored and get up.'

Another month passed, Fred was still staying in bed! I didn't know what to do. He didn't seem ill, or I would have called a doctor. One morning a couple of weeks later I took his breakfast in, and found he couldn't use his left arm, and he said his face felt funny. I phoned the doctor who said he would come after surgery. When he came he said Fred had suffered a slight stroke and said, 'He must not lie in bed, it's not helping him. He must also eat, and drink more liquid.' The doctor left, leaving a prescription for medication.

Needless to say, Fred would not get up. This went on and he had another stroke worse than the first. After a bit he seemed a little better, but still in bed. Christmas came and went, not a very happy one with Scrooge calling out for attention all the time.

At Easter he had the third stroke, which was a really bad one. After this he was absolutely helpless, I had to do everything for him. Still he would not try to eat or drink. The worst thing was, he would somehow roll out of bed. How he did this I'll never know. He used to roll out onto the floor about five times during the night. I used to have to pick him up somehow, and get him onto the bed. I pushed his bed to the wall one side, and put an armchair the other side, but still he would end up on the floor! All this was not doing my Angina a lot of good as you can imagine. I had been nursing him except for one visit a day from the District Nurse. I never got any help at all during the night when he was at his worst.

All this went on for three months, when three o'clock one morning he fell out of bed, and whilst struggling to get him back, I had an Angina attack, the worst pain I had had. I just had to let him drop. I crawled to the phone and called the doctor. When he came on I was hardly coherent. I could only say, 'He's on the floor, I am too, please come!' Fortunately the doctor recognized my voice and said, 'It's Mrs Holmes isn't it? I'll come straight away.' When he arrived he got Fred on to the bed and me onto an armchair, then phoned for an ambulance to take Fred to the hospital. 'Not before time,' my family and friends said.

I had to have three days' bed-rest before the doctor would allow me to go and see Fred. Apparently, in hospital Fred had started crying, never easing up. The doctor asked me, when I went to see Fred, why it was. I said I didn't know, but I had a sneaking suspicion why. He cried for the whole two weeks he was in there. The doctor who was treating him asked to see me. He then asked me – why? He said, 'I'm going to ask you some questions you will be cross with me for asking. Please don't be cross, your answers will help me assess your husband.' To my astonishment he asked me about my married life; was Fred normal in his habits, etc. I didn't want to tell him but thought he may throw a light on why Fred treated me so badly. After I told him, he said, 'I thought so. The reason Fred is crying and saying he's sorry is it's his conscience attacking him.'

I went every day and sat holding his hand. I don't think he knew I was there, he was hardly conscious. One afternoon I went in and sat as usual holding his hand, all of a sudden he opened his eyes and said, as best he could, 'I'm sorry Billie, I've been a swine to you. I should have put you first.' Not long after that he went into a coma, then just died. I left that hospital weighed down with sadness. Not for the loss of a husband, but for the poor creature who had just died, who had spoilt his, and my, life.

I think, as the hospital doctor thought, that his whole character had been changed by the treatment of his family when he was young. Well, I knew the family were not nice to him, as I often had to intervene in the early days of our marriage to save him stress caused by their treatment. I suppose he was having his own back by treating me the same.

After he died in October 1984, at the solicitors my daughter and I laughed when told how much he had left. 'You must be joking,' we said. He had only been giving me fifteen pounds a week for housekeeping! No holidays, no anything. Now at seventy with indifferent health I have all this money. I gave my daughter a nice chunk. Had several things done to the bungalow that were needed. So silly, I felt guilty when I bought something expensive. I kept going in the bank to ask my balance! It took me a long time to get used to spending money.

When all my affairs were in order I went on living quietly but now with enjoyment. I had enough money to do what I've always wanted to do, give nice presents to my friends and family, and no one telling me what a fool I was. I had a very nice conservatory built on the back of the house with access to the lounge. I keep it filled with flowering plants and lots of greenery. It's the nicest thing I have bought. When I am sitting in there I think of Fred. How he could have enjoyed things like this if only he had not been so mean. I sometimes think of the District Nurse who came in once a day to see Fred. She said, at one of the most difficult times, lifting Fred from the floor, 'How you must love this man, the way you nurse him, all the attention you give him.' I replied, 'But I don't love him, I would do the same for anybody as ill as this. I did love him once, but he killed that love. I vowed to stay in sickness and in health, till death do us part. That I have done.' We could have had such a good life together but he pushed it away. Such a waste!

Time for a holiday. My first one for years! My granddaughter Carolyn was now twenty years old, and had passed her driving test. I suggested that I hire a car and tour North Yorkshire. We could stay at the Hotel in Grassington and go out from there. Carolyn thought it a good idea, so I hired a Honda Jazz, a nice little car, very tough. We spent a lovely week together at the Grassington Hotel. The owner told me she had never seen a grandmother and granddaughter have such good fun together. Carolyn was, and still is, great fun!

Elaine and Allan had had some very good skiing holidays in France, Austria and Switzerland: always in February. This year they asked if I would like to go to Austria, not to ski, just sightseeing at Easter. I was more than keen. We booked in at the White Horse Inn in St Wolfgang. A wonderful hotel, the place unbelievable, the views, mountains and houses were out of this world and so quaint. I loved every moment. The thrill started when we got aboard the aircraft. This was the first time I had flown! I was so excited! Just like a child, but I couldn't help myself, it was wonderful. I could have flown hours, the journey was too short for me. We had a marvellous time, all too soon our time was up. I consoled myself by the thought of flying again when we returned though!

This was the year of The Hurricane. I had in my garden a very nice summer house, prettily furnished. The night before the hurricane I had put all the garden furniture plant stands, some of which were Victorian, and two pretty tables in there for the winter. During the night the summer house was flattened and everything in it smashed! I stood at the window in my nightdress at three o'clock in the morning, looking at utter devastation. Every tree and bush along the back of the garden was torn out, with fences down all around. Trees were laying across lawns. It was like looking at an earthquake! I stood alone and frightened wondering what I should do. The storm raged on sending roof tiles and chimneys flying. I had jumped out of bed when I heard the scream and whine of the whirlwind that had ravaged my garden. Not the ones either side strangely enough. *Dear God,* I thought, *what next*!

It took a month to tidy up the fences and other damage. Gone for good all the other things. There were still so many people worse off than me. I still had my house standing.

Christmas, now I was alone, was spent at Elaine's house. We always had a lovely time with Carolyn and Richard in the house. One day Allan, my son-in-law surprised me by saying, 'I know how you love the River Thames, Mum, so how would you like it if we three went on a cruise up the Thames for our next holiday?' I thought it was a lovely idea and said so. He got some brochures from the travel agents for us to browse through.

We decided to rent a cruiser, and start from Hampton Court and proceed as far as we could in three days, then turn back for the return journey. As there were three of us and two dogs, we thought we'd hire a six berth cruiser; we didn't want to be cramped.

I was so excited, the day to leave couldn't come soon enough. We hired our boat at Hampton Court and set off from there. Elaine was the skipper and Allan would deal with the locks we would encounter. I was the galley mate! It took a little while for Elaine to get going, then to our embarrassment we ran aground! With a little help from a passing boat we were afloat again. This was totally new to all three of us, we were quite excited. Elaine seemed to take to running the boat, I got a meal going in a well-appointed galley.

Night was falling so we found a mooring. In the night it started to rain. We awoke the next morning to find the rain pouring down! It did this every day and most nights. The only time the rain stopped was on a Wednesday afternoon when we moored at Windsor. Here we enjoyed sightseeing at the Castle and a meal in a very nice restaurant.

We passed through some lovely scenery; even the rain did not stop us enjoying ourselves. All along the banks of the Thames were beautiful houses with gardens down to the river's edge. Most had their own landing stage complete with boat moored alongside. We continued going through picturesque locks, past a beautiful small island called Temple Island. Along the river we saw lots of beautiful birds. Kingfishers, herons and swans were our constant companions all the way.

We travelled as far as Abingdon Lock and here we moored for the day. We went shopping, had lunch at a riverside inn and watched the students rowing. Next morning we turned around and made our way back, and it was still raining! We made our way back to Hampton Court, so we saw the other side of the river now.

It was a lovely restful holiday and made us appreciate our beautiful River Thames. I, for one, had a childhood dream come true. The rain never mattered to us. The three of us and the dogs enjoyed the whole trip, with never a cross word between us. The only anxious moment was when John the Labrador fell in the water between the boat and the towpath. Happily Allan managed to pull him out and all was well.

It was an uneventful trip back to Hampton Court where we left the boat and picked up the car to travel back to Thorpe Bay. We hope at another time to go further up the Thames.

I was still going to my Guild and giving talks. Going back to give my second talk was always nice. The people greeted me as if I was an old friend.

This year I hope to have another holiday. I'm going to ask Elaine to come with me to the Ashdown Forest. Elaine and Allan went skiing, this time in France with 'Club Med'. Later in August Elaine and I went to Ashdown forest and we stayed at Careys Manor House. On the journey down we took a picnic lunch. Once in the forest, we found an idyllic spot, a lovely little glade. Beautiful young birch trees, ferns, and to our joy, cowslips. It was so lovely. I wanted to dash home and alter my garden to look like this, so green and tranquil. There were wild ponies roaming the forest also. I did so enjoy that holiday. I'm not one for beaches and sunbathing.

Christmas at Elaine's was still very enjoyable, although Carolyn and Richard went off in the evening to friends. I couldn't bear New Year's Eve on my own so went to bed early!

I was still in touch with my friends in Tiptree and promised to visit them at Easter. Elaine and I planned a holiday in Jersey. As the holidays with Elaine always had to be in the school holidays, we missed their beautiful flower festival. We took a plane from Southend to Jersey. It's such a small island, pretty with some nice places to visit. I enjoyed Durrels Zoo.

I bought a lovely pearl necklace at a place where they made jewellery and other beautiful objects. We went late one night to the Corbiere light house to see the sunset. It was fabulous. It looked as if the sky was on fire, such vibrant colours. The sun a red ball in all this glowing orange, simply spectacular.

At the hotel we met a very nice couple from Hollingworth Lake, Lancashire, in England. The day we were to leave, our plane was found to be faulty so another one, a much smaller plane, was put at our disposal. The journey home was not very pleasant, the winds being very strong and our plane being rather small, we suffered from the turbulence. Some of the children were crying, the grown-ups looking worried! Not me, horrible me! I was enjoying it! I like rough weather when I'm sailing as well. We landed at Southend somewhat late.

We all had a nice Christmas at Elaine's. Carolyn was now married to a young man called Phil. She was now a computer programmer and they lived at Shoeburyness. Richard was now at the BBC Radio. I looked round at my little family with pride and great love. This was all I ever wanted: a happy family life.

In March I went with my friend Sheila to a dinner for Mr Teddy Taylor, celebrating ten years as our MP held at the House of Commons.

Unfortunately, the Poll Tax Rioters were very active that night. The police directed all the traffic to other routes. All the bridges were closed. Everywhere was packed with people, shouting and brandishing weapons. Some had pieces of stout wood, alight at one end. Cars were turned over, some set on fire! These men were surging around our coach and I thought they would push it over. We were so scared. Our driver gradually eased the coach along. Some policemen helped us off. We set off in little groups all huddled together close to the railings. Before we could get to the gates, my friend and I were stopped by a burly man who was unwashed and unshaven and who had a lighted piece of wood in his hand. 'Get out you Bastards,' he shouted. I thought he was going to push the burning wood in my face. I went rigid with fear! Thank God he left us. We staggered on till we got to the gates. The police were only opening them just enough to allow one person at a time through.

At long last we were all assembled inside. None of us looking as good as when we set out! Thank God no one was hurt, only very frightened. What an experience. We were two hours late sitting down to our meal. The meal was excellent even so. I had to keep my coat on all evening I was so cold. I suppose it was the shock. It was the first time I had known real terror!

I had had a very traumatic five months this year and was still far from well.

One Sunday morning in May I collapsed, ending up in the Intensive Care Unit in Rochford Hospital for seven days. As usual I fought my way through this with my unquenchable Cockney spirit.

Home again, but I had to attend a Cardiac Clinic every month for one year. This year cannot pass quickly enough for me, so I will ignore some of it. In September I went with my friend Sheila on a 'Luxury Train Tour' to Scotland. I had always wanted to go to Scotland, as my maternal grandmother was born in Edinburgh. I fell in love with all of it. We went to the Isle of Skye and to the Orkneys. While we were there seven of our warships were moored in the bay. It was a beautiful sight. I really enjoyed the boat trip to the Orkneys. It was so very rough, my kind of sea! Sheila wasn't so happy, she is not very fond of the sea. All around us were mountains covered with heather. I took lots of photographs.

We also spent a night in a wonderful hotel half-way up a mountain. We arrived in the afternoon just as a wedding party was arriving. It was like a film set. All the men were in kilts, and the ladies looked wonderful in white dresses and sashes. Such colour everywhere. The pipers were in full force as well.

The next morning after breakfast we all assembled in the hall waiting for the train manager to arrive to escort us back to our train. This had been left in a siding for cleaning and replenishment. When the manager arrived I said to Sheila, 'My God, look at his face!' He was ashen, he then told us that last night another train, an Express, had gone into the back of ours and had done quite a lot of damage! If we had been in it! After some waiting we were driven back to our train and saw for ourselves the escape we had.

Off again, this time to spend a day at Edinburgh. For years I had been buying material from a very good shop called 'Jenners' by post, now I thought I'd buy in person. It certainly was a super store. I loved this holiday and would like to see more of Scotland. I would dearly love to visit every place in my beloved British Isles.

I still had to take things easy, so for the rest of the year I planned to sew and sit in the garden. I re-planned the garden with help, but I needed to do more than this, I was getting bored. Inactivity isn't something I enjoy.

On my seventy-eighth birthday I sat down and took stock of my life. What I had done, and what I would like to do. I had done most things I'd wanted to do, but one thing remained. I had never forgotten my idol Amy Johnson, and how I had envied her flying. So, I thought, there's not much exertion in flying surely. Why not give it a whirl!

Well, with me, no sooner the thought than the deed. I looked up the

Southend Airport number and rang them. I got through to 'Sky Lane', the flying school, and asked the girl who answered if they had someone to teach me to fly. She asked when I would like to come. I answered, 'Now!' She said, 'I'll see if there's an instructor available.' After a minute she said, 'Yes, Jan is here, can you be here in half an hour?'

Gosh! I rang for a taxi, rushed around the house locking up. I was ready. I got to the airport on time and after a bit, found Sky Lane, went in and said who I was. A nice looking tall fellow who was lounging in a chair, said, 'I'm Jan and you are . . .?' 'Billie,' I replied. 'OK Billie let's get started.'

He took me to a small room at the end of the building, which had maps on every wall, and a large model of a Cessna 115. He took me through a pre-flight briefing, demonstrating by way of the model, all parts of the plane. This took about half an hour. We then plotted our route, and went outside to do a pre-flight check. Every single screw and rivet was tested, fuel and oil checked as well as the flaps, lights, etc. Not a thing left to chance! Now we get to the cockpit and I'm in the pilot's seat. We then proceed to check all the dials in front of us, checking they tallied with his clipboard. All well. Jan then switched on, revved up a little, and showed me how to go left or right with the foot pedals. Not like a car.

We are on the runway. Jan told me to taxi slowly down to a slip lane, where I would have to wait for the Air Control to tell me when I could take off. I was so impatient to get in the air!

At last permission! Well, Jan told me to give a bit more throttle and run to the left. I did this and he said, 'Pull the throttle right out and pull the stick back.' I did all this, and to my delight I saw the nose of the aircraft slowly pointing upwards. I'm afraid I was now shrieking with delight, not at all the behaviour of a woman of seventy-eight years!

We gradually gathered speed and height. You cannot imagine the utter thrill of soaring in to the sky. Oh gosh, at long last I was here doing what I had wanted all my life. Oh Amy, thank you for inspiring me to do this.

Jan was an excellent instructor, he told me to turn to the left and follow the coastline. After this we turned in towards land and flew all over Essex. I was so happy, no chest pains, no hassle, just utter peace combined with excitement. I was in seventh heaven. If only I had been a man I would have been in the RAF and I hope a pilot in a Spitfire. Well, as always, the hour had come to an end too quickly. Such a swift hour.

As we walked back to the office Jan said, 'Billie, you're a natural flyer. From the moment you put your hands on the stick I knew. You were so relaxed and happy I knew you'd be fine. Most people are very tense and uptight.' When we got to the office I paid, and booked another lesson, I was totally hooked.

That same day I had a hair appointment at 3 p.m. and a doctor's appointment at 5 p.m. I went into the hairdresser's, and Loretta, the owner, said, 'Gosh, Billie what have you been up to? You look fabulous.' I told them and they didn't believe me at first, so I showed them the receipt. There was a chorus of 'I couldn't do that,' or 'I'd have a fit if I was asked to fly a plane.'

At 5 p.m. I turned up at the doctor's. I just about got into his room when he said, 'Good Lord, Mrs Holmes what on earth have you been up to? You look on top of the world.' I said, 'I've been flying. Me! Flying, can you imagine!' I asked him why I didn't have any pain in my chest. He said, 'Because you were totally relaxed, no harassment, just sheer joy.' I said, 'Next time I'll take my lunch and make a day of it!' He laughed and said, 'Anything so long as it makes you feel like this.'

I was on a high for three days. I did my usual things at home during the week but longing for the next flight. I envied every pilot in the planes that flew overhead. I would just stand in the street gazing until they were out of sight.

Jan had left the school and I now had John who said, 'Let's follow the Thames to London and have a look at the new bridge they are building.' We did just that, it looked lovely from the air. That morning I had not brought my camera, such a pity. Going back home, John said that we would land at another part of the runway. I flew on as told, then all of a sudden as I was coming down I stupidly looked down. To my horror I saw the chimneys of the bungalows beneath me. They looked so close I was scared. I shouted, 'Oh no, I'll kill them! John, you fly.' He took control and finished the landing for me. John said, 'What was that a about? You were doing perfectly well.'

'I just felt I was too low over those bungalows. I was so afraid I might kill someone,' I said, through my tears, 'I'm so sorry.' He gave my hand a squeeze and said, 'OK let's forget it.' A week after, I was fully recovered from the fright. John and I set off for a Flying Club at Earls Colne. Before I took off, we phoned the club asking for permission to land. They gave the OK, I told them our Estimated Time of Arrival and we set off. It was very nicely situated. I landed where I was directed to go, and then went to the Control Tower to pay our landing fees. There were three men working on charts. John knew one of them and said, 'May I introduce my Co-pilot Billie Holmes.' It was a proud moment for me. He told them how good I was, a born flyer, he said, and added, 'I'd like you chaps to try to persuade her to go for a Flying Licence.' I burst in before they could say anything, 'I'm too old at seventy-eight to pass any exams. So long as I know I can fly, that's all that matters. I don't want certificates. I wouldn't want to fly on my own anyway.'

On the way home I landed OK, no problems. It was a lovely flight that day, weather perfect. My great thrill was to be up in the clouds. It's another world, when I'm up there I feel so insignificant, yet part of it all, I could do anything.

I'd been flying once a week for five weeks now; I didn't want to do anything else. I would have gone every day, but some days it cost me over a hundred pounds. One has to try to be sensible. I took my camera for one flight, took snaps of the front and back of my bungalow. We then shot away over the water making for Canterbury in Kent. The sun was shining, it was a glorious morning. All of a sudden I saw the Cathedral, with the sun on it. It was a wondrous sight, it shone like gold. We flew around a bit then started for home.

We were out in the country by now, and all of a sudden John said, 'How about a mock Mayday?' I, never stopping to think, said, 'OK, what do I do?' In the distance there was a large field, empty of cattle. To this he pointed and said, 'As we haven't got a permit to land here, we must dive low and then quickly come up again.' 'OK,' said I. John immediately turned off the engine. My God, the propeller was hardly turning, the plane wobbled a bit then glided. I caught her then, and kept her straight till I dived almost to the ground. John turned the engine on, I gave her full throttle and shot into the air gaining height rapidly. Whew! that was exciting. I turned to John and said, 'That was the most exciting thing I have ever done!'

On the way home I was on cloud nine. It's funny; I didn't feel afraid at all, so intent was I in what I was doing. It was after, when I felt very shaky, I wanted to cry. How daft can you get. John shouted, 'What a gal! I wish I had known you as a girl.' I retorted by saying. 'You were not even born when I was a girl!' I went home that day wanting to shout from the roof-top. I just could not believe I had the nerve to do such a thing. Of course I had John with me so there was no real danger. So, now I can fly. What next?